recrea†ed

how Jesus transforms our story

shane callicutt

Copyright © 2016 by Shane Callicutt

All rights reserved. No part of this publication may be reproduced, distributed, or transmitted in any form or by any means, including photocopying, recording, or other electronic or mechanical methods, without the prior written permission of the publisher, except in the case of brief quotations embodied in critical reviews and certain other noncommercial uses permitted by copyright law. For permission requests, contact the author via the website listed below.

Shane Callicutt
www.shaneshack.com

Scripture quotations are from the ESV® Bible (The Holy Bible, English Standard Version®), copyright © 2001 by Crossway, a publishing ministry of Good News Publishers. Used by permission. All rights reserved.

Thank you to Julie and Cathy for reviewing this in your spare time. Thank you to Sharon for your editing skills. All three of you made a significant contribution to my thought process and momentum as I wrote.

I'm grateful for all of the unnamed people in this book who have shaped me through the years. Whether you realize it or not, Jesus used you for great good.

Special thanks to my wife, Radene, who put up with me asking her to read things when she was half way asleep or kind of busy. I don't promise to stop doing that… but I do promise to try to never embarrass you in anything I write.

contents

Introduction	1
Chapter 1: Adopted	5
Chapter 2: Bullied	23
Chapter 3: Saved	43
Chapter 4: Forgiveness	63
Chapter 5: People Pleaser	81
Chapter 6: Fight	101
Chapter 7: Our Victor	123
In Closing	139

introduction

"*The details of my life are quite inconsequential. Very well, where do I begin?*"[1] Dr. Evil couldn't have been more wrong. The details of life are *very* consequential. The details of life are the things that shape our character. They shape our disposition. In the classic argument of *nature versus nurture*, nurture is tenacious. While it's true that genetics map out the building blocks for our personalities, our tendencies, and our dispositions, it is *nurture* that helps us integrate those things successfully, first into family life, then into community life. Nature may give us what we have to work with, but nurture teaches us how to work with what we have.

If you understand the details, you understand a great deal about the person. My life isn't some spectacular story worthy of a Hollywood movie. I didn't rise from great adversity into any kind of position or power. I'm white, married with two children, nearly-forty, middle-class, I live in a small town in the Missouri Ozarks where I serve as the worship pastor at my church, and do photography and IT work on the side. Not really much to see here, but like I said, it's the details that really tell the story.

I'm not writing this book because my life is some great story that needs to be told. I'm writing this because *God's story* in my life needs to be told! Nature and nurture play their role in everyone who is born. But for those who trust Jesus Christ for salvation, a third more powerful party enters the picture, and he is greater than both nature and nurture. He transforms our stories into something that neither nature nor nurture could have accomplished. His presence in my life is changing an ordinary story into something extraordinary.

So while, the details of life may *seem* inconsequential, pay attention. Most of us are ordinary. We have ordinary circumstances, ordinary jobs, with sub-ordinary pay, and we live in ordinary homes. We never think of ourselves in extraordinary terms. Boring details dominate. But when Jesus enters the picture, if you let him, boring details become transforming opportunities. God's goal is to *recreate* us into someone like Jesus. The difficulties of life, the hardships we endure end up being a servant in your greater transformation, and life is never *ordinary* again.

This isn't a play by play of my life from birth to the present. I've only highlighted the thread of redemption that God has woven in me through the years in the hope that you

introduction

will find it helpful. I've been as careful as I know how to protect the people I mention in this book. I'm not writing this to take cheap shots at people from my past. I've only used names where there's no risk involved in doing so. I'm also keenly aware that this book may (hopefully) be read by people who have known me my whole life. To you I say, thank you for your friendship and contribution into my life.

Let me also add that I'm sharing some things in this book that up until now I've only shared with my wife, Radene. If you grew up with me, you may find yourself in some of these stories. I've done my best to protect your privacy. One of the chapters is about my experiences with being bullied, and while I had to write about people who bullied me, you remained nameless. I've written this book to glory in my weakness and bring glory to my amazing Savior, not to expose the failures of people around me. His grace has been more than sufficient for me!

It is my hope that you find encouragement as you read this book. I hope that my hardships, my obstacles, help you see how your hardships and obstacles don't have to be for nothing. In the hands of Christ, trials and obstacles are tools that are shaping believers into people who demonstrate the power and glory of God. It ultimately isn't about where you came from, nature or nurture, but it's about where you are going and how God can step in and supersede the powers that have shaped you. He will transform your story from the beginning to the end in ways you never could have on your own.

recreated

References:
1. *Austin Powers: International Man of Mystery*. Dir. Jay Roach. Perf. Mike Meyers, Elizabeth Hurley, Michael York. New Line Cinema, 1997. Film.

adopted

"For I am God, and there is no other; I am God, and there is none like me, declaring the end from the beginning and from ancient times things not yet done, saying, 'My counsel shall stand, and I will accomplish all my purpose,'" (Isaiah 46:9-10 ESV)

When I think back on my life, as far back as I can remember, I frequently have to throw up my hands and say, *"Lord, only you know."* My sisters and I were adopted when I was three. I don't really remember life before my adoption. All I have are pictures. Pictures of a life I don't remember. Not that any of us can remember those early years with much clarity, but in my case that part of life was fundamentally different. Mom and dad were different. Fortunately, we were adopted by our grandparents, so the change wasn't as dramatic as many adoptions, where the children go to people they never knew before.

The truth is for a long time I didn't want to know. I don't know why. It's not that I didn't have questions. I just never bothered to ask them. Maybe at a deeper level, I sensed that digging into the *why* of the adoption might cause a larger rift in a family that was already hurting. I've never been one for conflict. I hate arguing. I despise fighting. Even today, I value the peace of my home above *many* things. There are only a blessed few things for which I will sacrifice my family's peace. I have protected my daughters from a lot of family drama over the years so they can enjoy the innocence of just loving their family.

Before I go any further, to minimize confusion, let me lay down some terms and ground rules. Discussing a situation where your grandparents become your parents can become confusing where names are concerned. When referring to my birth parents, I will use the terms *mom* and *dad*. When referring to my adoptive parents (grandparents) I will use the terms *mamma* and *daddy*. Any other mother or father figures mentioned along the way will have the usual prefix *step* added.

Also, I want to strive to keep the fifth commandment: honor your father and mother. In a case where I have two of each, that can be challenging. I believe it's important that even as adults, we strive to keep honoring our parents in the Lord. Being a parent, I am keenly aware that there are no perfect parents. Having been a child, and having children of my own, I know that there are no perfect children. Therefore, this is not going to be a place where I air the dirty laundry of my family. Every family has dirty laundry, and though the messes maybe different, we're all equally loaded. I won't be endorsing one parent over another, I won't be saying this person tells the truth and this one doesn't.

The truth is I don't have a cohesive story. As I've gotten older and more details have come to light, I've tried to put the pieces together into a neatly organized jigsaw, only to find out that some of the pieces don't fit well. Some of them will never fit. I've made peace with this. I don't need a perfectly assembled puzzle to love my family. In my heart, I believe all of my parents have striven to be truthful and do what's right. Therefore, if the stories don't line up, I'm chalking it up to different motives and perspectives on what happened. The adoption happened and that's an irrefutable, unchangeable fact. I can either spend enormous time and energy trying to make sense of it, or I can embrace the mess, and just love my family. Because here's the truth: no matter what, no matter who, no matter how, my family has loved me.

My mom sacrificed much to let go of her right to raise her children. For thirteen long years, early eighties to mid nineties, she was married to a man who threatened her and threatened our safety (me and my sisters) if she were to ever leave or cross him the wrong way. But whenever she could, she would pour into my life. One simple, but profound thing she taught me was to *read the book* whenever I couldn't figure out how to do something. Any skill I have related to computers, or anything that can be learned from reading can be traced back to my mom refusing to do it for me and making me dig it out of a book. I called her many times when I couldn't figure it out, and to my frustration the first words out of her mouth would often be, "Did you read the book?" She did what she could to love me under her circumstances. She always made sure that I knew she loved me, and I always knew that she did.

My mamma and daddy, because they adopted, they sacrificed what should've been a peaceful, restful retirement. Daddy taught me a good work ethic. He taught me what it meant to have excellent character. My *dad*, shortly after my mom divorced him, stopped coming around. Thankfully, daddy stepped into that role and helped me become a man. He would frequently sit in his chair and read his Bible. He was humble, but never short of an opinion if you asked him. He was always teaching me how to do things outside, though I wasn't always a willing participant. I told him one day that work is boring, and his reply was exasperated and stern: "It's not always supposed to be fun!" Cut to the chase; that was my daddy.

Mamma always made sure we were well fed, ready for school, and stocked with supplies. She worked, but she always seemed to have time and energy for the extra things that kids end up doing at school. She was tenacious. She still is. Even today, in her eighties, mamma still has a lot of fight left in her. She's had many obstacles with her health in her latter years, particularly arthritis, but has pressed through them. After my sister, Kelly, passed away in 2013, mamma took in her sixteen-year-old son. She pressed through her

adopted

physical problems to make sure that he had a place to live and rest his head. She's taught me endurance and tenacity. In the midst of trial and adversity, she never stopped loving the Lord and loving us.

What about my dad? Like I said earlier, he basically stopped coming around after mom divorced him. I have a vague memory of him buying me a Mellow Yellow, but I don't remember his face. I just remember his pick-up truck. But that's not the end. When I graduated from high school, I received a letter and a gift from him. In the letter, he fell on the old adage, *you can lead a horse to water, but you can't make him drink.* Honestly, I've never had one moment of ill feelings toward him. And in some ways, because I know how my emotions work, I think I know why he stopped coming. The longer you stay away, the more embarrassed you get that you've allowed so much time to pass, therefore the less inclined you become to come around. It gets harder to go and easier to keep distance as time goes on. Though we did ultimately reconnect, sadly it faded once again after a few years. I moved to Colorado, got married, started planting roots out there with my wife, and was only visiting Mississippi once a year. We lost touch again. But if he called me today, I'd try to pick up the pieces afresh.

Now that the players are in place, what about this adoption? I only have one word: providential. The first thing you read in this chapter was Isaiah 46:9-10. "I am God, and there is none like me, *declaring the end from the beginning.*" No matter how I look at this, God's hand has been at work leading and directing the flow and direction of my life. It doesn't matter whose version of the adoption I embrace, even if I rejected all of them and decided for myself what happened, it wouldn't matter. God knows my beginning from my end, and add to that, he knows every intimate detail in between!

> O LORD, you have searched me and known me! You know when I sit down and when I rise up; you discern my thoughts from afar. *You search out my path and my lying down and are acquainted with all my ways* . . . Your eyes saw my unformed substance; *in your book were written, every one of them, the days that were formed for me, when as yet there was none of them.* (Psalm 139:1-3, 16 ESV, emphasis added)

The adoption happened as a part of the plan that God had for bringing me, and my sisters, into his family. You may wonder, as I have, why did it take such measures? Couldn't God have saved us, no matter what? In short, if God works it out a certain way, then it *is* the best way, no matter how we feel about it. But more to the issue, the problem with narrowing it down to that question is that it's too small of a question. The situation, as most are, is bigger than one life. There were multiple people involved, all of whom God had reasons and purposes for shaping things they way he shaped them. So, in many ways we may have been the adoptees, but we were in no way the only ones impacted.

adopted

God has redemptive purposes in *everything* he does, for *everyone* affected by his actions. As painful as the adoption was for my mom, God had a redemptive purpose in mind for her as she endured letting go of her children. God had a redemptive purpose in mind for mamma and daddy as they worked hard to raise a second generation of children. I don't know what it was for them. That's something between them and the Lord Jesus. Whether or not they ever discovered God's purpose in all of it, again, is something I cannot say. All I can tell you is how the adoption affected me, and it was impactful.

I received a godly heritage, as did my sisters. Church was never an optional activity. Unless we were sick or traveling, we went to church on Sundays. Growing up in the 80s and 90s in northeast Mississippi meant it was a safe assumption that you were attending church somewhere. People who didn't were still somewhat passively branded rebels and sinners. Growing up, we attended three different churches, and one of them twice. Temple Baptist Church is where I was until I was around eight, and it is where we returned when I was thirteen, so I count it as my *home church*.

Looking back on my formative years in church I usually think of Temple. My great grandfather, King Callicutt (yes, that is his real name) helped form that church (to what extent is unclear) when it splintered from Myrtle Baptist Church back in the 1940s. Our family has roots there, I suppose. There's a tradition in our family of faithfulness to God and to his church.

God's faithfulness to me, before I even knew him, came in part through the agency of human adoption. It paved the way for my spiritual adoption. From a certain perspective it was a foreshadowing the beautiful work that God was going to do in my life. Adoption is a powerful force. Roman law gave adoption a stronger legal bond than that of natural born children, and this historically continued to be the case in many Western nations.[1] The human adoption I experienced, while powerful and impactful, was only a glimpse at what adoption entailed in the ancient world.

Timothy Keller offers a detailed description of what adoption looked like in Roman culture.[2] Adoption normally happened when an affluent adult found himself with no heir to his estate. What followed is he would adopt an heir. That heir could be a child, a youth, or an adult. When we think of adoption, we usually think about adopting children, but the Roman idea was much more robust. It had more to do with the legalities that surrounded wealth and what happened to that wealth when the owner dies than with compassion, although I'm sure compassion had a role.

Keller notes four things that would happen in Roman adoption. First the debts and obligations of the one being adopted were paid off. Second, the adoptee would receive a new name and became an instant heir of everything the father possessed. Third, from that moment the new father became liable for all of his new son's actions, including future debts and crimes. And fourth, the new son had new obligations to honor and please his new father.

> For you did not receive the spirit of slavery to fall back into fear, but you have received the Spirit of *adoption* as sons, by whom we cry, "Abba! Father!" (Romans 8:15 ESV, emphasis added)

Your debts and obligations are paid off. When I was adopted I was too young to have any debts. But in Roman times, if the adoptee was old enough to have incurred financial or societal debts, the adopting father would take ownership of those debts. If the adopted son owed money, that debt became the father's debt. If that adopted son had been disgraced, the father would take that disgrace upon himself. Adoption wasn't just the giving of a family name, a place to call home, and an inheritance, it was also the father taking ownership of the shame, debt, and guilt of the adoptee! In addition, adoption in the ancient world was a stronger legal bond than natural parents. Once you were adopted, you could *never* be un-adopted. You could never separate yourself from your new family, and your new father could never disown you. It was an ultimate, final decision, no take-backs.

What an incredible picture of the grace of God in electing to adopt me! I may have been too young to have financial or societal debts when mamma and daddy adopted me, but I was born a sinner! I may not have been that old, but I was already pushing my sisters down when they tried to walk. I was already disobeying. I was already lying to stay out of trouble. I was already hiding when I did something I knew was wrong. Little sinner that I was! And yet, even as I continued to pile up debt on top of debt for fifteen years, God still loved me and extended his grace to me! Adopted! But not only is the accrued debt from my past covered by adoption, my future debts are also covered because once I'm adopted by the Father I'll *never* cease to be God's son!

You receive a new name and become an instant heir of everything God has. When I was adopted, I received a new name. My last name went from Kyle to Callicutt. And when my last name became Callicutt, whatever Herman Callicutt had, I now had. Even today, I have some of his things. When he passed away, what had been implicitly mine, actually became mine. And those things that I received from him, now implicitly belong to my children. When we are born again, we are adopted into God's family and we receive a new name. Where we were once an *enemy*, now our name is *son*.

> The nations shall see your righteousness,
> > and all the kings your glory,
> and you shall be called by a *new name*
> > that the mouth of the LORD will give.
> (Isaiah 62:2 ESV, emphasis added)

Now here's a shocker. The inheritance we receive as adopted sons is the same inheritance that Jesus Christ, God's only begotten, natural son, will receive. What an amazing promise, because Jesus will literally inherit everything! If you can see it, touch it, feel it, Jesus will inherit it. And so will we as fellow heirs with him.

> The Spirit himself bears witness with our spirit that we are children of God, and if children, then heirs—heirs of God and fellow heirs with Christ, provided we suffer with him in order that we may also be glorified with him. (Romans 8:16-17 ESV)

How exciting is it to know that every galaxy in the universe, every atom that makes up every star and planet is part of your inheritance in Christ? But the most exciting, and the thing that will keep us satisfied for all eternity, is the unhindered, undiluted access we will have to the Father for all eternity. The Trinity, the three-in-one God-head, the Father, the Son, the Holy Spirit, *in one sense*, will forever be altered to allow all his adopted sons access into that perfect fellowship. More than owning every square inch of creation, having access to the pure unadulterated joy that exists in the fellowship of the God-head will satisfy us for all eternity future, just as it satisfied the Trinity in all of eternity past. You cannot fully wrap your finite mind around it, but it is the lion's share of the glory that will be revealed to us!

> For I consider that the sufferings of this present time are not worth comparing with the glory that is to be revealed to us. (Romans 8:18 ESV)

The new father became liable for all of his new son's actions, including future debts and crimes. In the Roman sense, that meant that this new father would be legally responsible for his new son's future indiscretions. If he stole money or property, the father could be held responsible along with the son for the crime. If at any time I decided to break the law, while I lived with mamma and daddy, the legal power of the adoption would've made them legally responsible for my actions. Depending on what I did, they would be financially responsible to make restitution for my crimes.

God the Father is no different. When he adopted me, he took responsibility for all of my past, present, and future sins and trespasses. Even as I sit here and write this, my mind is flooded with the sins that I committed over the course of the last few days. I was born again in 1992. Today is 2015. Those sins I committed over the last few days, God assumed legal responsibility for in 1992. What does that mean? How does that work itself out? Why would a holy God take responsibility for my sins? Look to the cross of Christ.

The cross of Christ is how God took responsibility for my sins. The ugly, yet beautiful exchange that happened on the cross is that all of my unrighteousness, all of my sins, all of my trespasses were placed upon Jesus as he took the punishment I deserved for those sins. Jesus willingly took the punishment that I deserved and became my restitution. He became my payment. He became my sacrifice. The death I should've paid for my sins, he died.

For our sake he made him to be sin who knew no sin, so that in him we might become the righteousness of God. (2 Corinthians 5:21 ESV)

Christ redeemed us from the curse of the law by becoming a curse for us—for it is written, "Cursed is everyone who is hanged on a tree"— (Galatians 3:13 ESV)

Jesus *became* sin. Jesus *became* a curse. He became something that by nature he was not. How? By choice! He chose to take our sins. That's why those sins I have done over the past few days were covered from the day I was born again in 1992. Why did he do this? He did it for our sake out of his great love. Did he have to? Certainly not! We were the reason Jesus had to die! That makes us an accomplice to his murder! But the fact that he chose us anyway, demonstrates his amazing grace, his immeasurable love. It was in this incredible act of love that God took responsibility for my sin, placed those sins upon Jesus, and in exchange placed the righteousness of Christ upon me so I can *become the righteousness of God* in Christ.

but God shows his love for us in that while we were still sinners, Christ died for us. (Romans 5:8 ESV)

And that isn't the end. He also takes responsibility for my sins by transforming me into someone who thinks, speaks, and acts like Jesus. By giving me the righteousness of Christ, something I could never earn, he obligates himself to transform me into someone I could never become. If God gave me the righteousness of Christ as a gift, but then never bothered to ensure that I actually started living like Christ, he would dishonor his Son and dishonor his own name. What good is there in giving someone great wealth, who didn't earn it, doesn't know how to manage it, doesn't understand the responsibility of owning it? Not only would they ruin their own lives, but also the lives of many who surround them. And the giver of that wealth would be held responsible for enabling this disaster.

God won't allow his name to be drug through the mud, so he takes the responsibility of ensuring that I am transformed into a person who bears the likeness of Christ.

> Now may the God of peace himself *sanctify you completely*, and may your whole spirit and soul and body be kept blameless at the coming of our Lord Jesus Christ. He who calls you is faithful; *he will surely do it*. (1 Thessalonians 5:23-24 ESV, emphasis added)

The new son had new obligations to honor and please his new father. Whether I realized it or not, my adoption had a profound impact on my conduct as a child. When I look back, I remember many passed opportunities to get into fights. I remember many moments where I had a choice to make: do what I knew was right, or do what I wanted to do. Of course

adopted

I didn't *always* make the right choice, but I was considered a *good* kid, so clearly there was a weight of good choices that gave me that label. But all those passed opportunities had one common theme. I did not want to disappoint my daddy. I didn't understand it at the moment, but as time has passed, and my understanding has matured, I see the great sacrifice of *all* my parents and it has caused my love for them to skyrocket. I want to make them proud today more than ever. I want to honor the memory of my daddy by being a man of excellent character. I want mom *and* mamma to smile ear to ear when they think of the man I have become.

There is something innate within us that obliges us to please when we become aware of someone's sacrifice on our behalf. I hesitate to characterize it as an obligation because we tend think of obligations as payments in return. In my mind the word *obligation* carries a coldness to it that reduces my response to a calculated return on investment. It's so much more, but I can't think of a better word to describe the gravity of my response. The desire is so great, so weighty, that I *must* do what I can to honor them.

Explode that out to the sacrifice that God made to adopt me, and the gravity of the obligation requires my entire life! Christ bore all my sins, died my death, and then resurrected my resurrection; fully purchasing for me an eternity that was beyond my reach. He has done it all and all I have had to do is believe by faith and repent. How simple, how glorious!

As you begin to realize that every day God's grace has covered your sins afresh, and when you begin to take note of how much sin penetrates and permeates your whole being, and then how powerless you are to stop it on your own, the worship begins to flow! The gratitude begins to pour out! I'm not a huge advocate of getting wrapped up in focusing on how sinful we are, but there is a healthy recognition of how depraved we are that propels us into greater worship. If you never think about your sin, you will slowly forget how desperately you need a Savior. On the other hand, if all you ever think about is how sinful you are, you will neglect the authority that the Savior has invested in you to overcome sin. Both cases lead to forgetfulness about Jesus in one way or another, and lead to a self-centered idolatry where you are the center of your universe. Keeping my eyes fixed on Jesus has done more for my battle with sin than any scheme I've concocted to stop sinning.

My adoption into the family of God has provided for me an eternal source of authority, power, joy, happiness, forgiveness, and purpose that comes from only one source: Jesus crucified and resurrected. He is my authority. He is my power. He is my joy. He is my happiness. He is my forgiveness. He is my purpose. Adoption has not only changed my destination, but it has changed the journey that will lead me there. I am forever transformed, starting fresh every new morning!

adopted

Though you have not seen him, you love him. Though you do not now see him, you believe in him and rejoice with joy that is inexpressible and filled with glory, obtaining the outcome of your faith, the salvation of your souls. (1 Peter 1:8-9 ESV)

References
1. W. M. Ramsay, *A Historical Commentary on St. Paul's Epistle to the Galatians*, Baker Book House, Grand Rapids, MI, reprinted 1979.
2. Timothy Keller, *Galatians for You*, The Good Book Company, Purcellville, VA, 2013.

bullied

I'm a big guy. *I have what doctors like to call a little bit of a weight problem.*[1] Even as a child, I was heavy. Once upon a time back in the day, I desperately wanted to play basketball, so I tried out every year from seventh grade all the way through my senior year. I practiced nearly every day. I got better, but I never really was varsity material. One consequence of my basketball pursuit was that I lost a lot of weight, and as I did my athleticism improved. I was never a six-pack, but I went from being big and overweight, to just being big. I was a big white kid whose only advantage on the court was strength and size because I simply could not jump. Yet, coach kept playing me in positions where I needed vertical ability. No wonder my basketball career kept stalling! In all truth, I had athleticism, but my mind just wasn't grasping the game like it needed to in order to play varsity.

You'd think that being a big, strong young man, despite my basketball setbacks, I would have the world on my plate. You'd think wrong. There's a dark side to this story that I haven't really talked very openly about as an adult. It stains almost every memory of I have of school, from kindergarten to high school. Painful, heart wrenching, and seldom talked about, I experienced loads and loads of rejection during school.

It all started in kindergarten. My memory is hazy, but what I do remember clearly is being pushed up against the chain link fence that surrounded our playground. It was my first fight and I lost. Kindergarten was the first place that I really remember meeting new kids and making new friends. This guy didn't want to be my friend. I don't even know why. Was I too fat? Was I too obnoxious? Was it both? All I remember clearly about it is how I felt. Everyone was watching, everyone walked away, and I was left there standing against that fence. Rejected.

Fast forward. Second grade baseball. I was still a big kid with a weight problem, but I wanted to play baseball. Who could fault a young fat kid for wanting to do something physically active, right? As it turns out, baseball bored me to death. All I cared about was batting. I hated playing the outfield. And on top of that, I played right field. Anyone who knows anything about baseball knows that right field is where players go to wait while everyone else is involved in winning the game. That is until a left handed kid gets up to bat, then it's all nerves and shouting from the dugout because I'm drawing pictures in the dirt while the ball is heading right for me.

bullied

All I wanted to do was bat and run those bases. As I remember it, I wasn't too bad at batting, but because I was overweight, I wasn't as great at running. There was a kid on our team who was simply ruthless with me. He called me names while I ran the bases. "Turkey!" "Fatty!" "Slow poke!" I honestly don't know what I did to him to make him dislike me so much. It seemed somewhat out of the blue that he began tormenting me like this. Maybe he just didn't like fat kids. But regardless of his reason, those words hurt. They really started to do a number on me. And rather than push me toward a confrontation, I tried befriending him. Of course, this didn't work.

The taunting continued. The kid from my baseball team became a frequent offender. Then his friends began chiming in. Essentially, a small group of boys seemed to make it their mission in life to make fun of me and reject me. This continued through junior high, through much of high school, and go figure, they were on the basketball team that I so badly wanted to join. I am not exaggerating when I say that I would have days at school where kids I don't even really know that well would say horrible things to me. One instance that comes to mind was around my sixth grade year. I was walking, minding my own business, when someone on the junior high side of the school yard yelled at me, "Nobody likes you!"

I was being bullied. And the sad thing about all of this is that all I wanted was to be accepted for who I was. I was not a violent kid; I didn't want to fight. In fact, there were times where I was ready to fight, but the fear of disappointing my dad kept me from fighting. My dad never really taught me how to fight, and led me to believe that I would be in huge trouble if I got in fights. I remember getting into a fight with the neighbor kid one time, got in big trouble with my parents, and then I had to call his mother and apologize. Sometimes, I really felt powerless.

Don't get me wrong, I had friends, and they, to this day, are great friends. I could retreat into my small circle of friends and find comfort, but you can't stay there all the time. When I tried sports, when I tried clubs, anything extracurricular would always bring me around the people who wanted nothing to do with me, and they ensured that I knew that.

It was a vicious cycle I was in. The harder I tried to find acceptance with these people, the harder they pushed me away with bullying and ridicule. Plus, because I was trying so hard, sometimes my behavior would become obnoxious, thus not really helping my cause. As a kid, I couldn't resolve the problem in my head of why I needed the approval of these people so badly. Why did I so desperately want to fit in? Why was it so important for me to connect socially with these people? I'm no sociologist or psychologist, but looking back on my life, here's a few observations from my saved, adult self.

Though adoption had a profound impact on my life, there is an issue of abandonment that lingered in my heart. Why? For a child who neither had the full story nor the emotional intelligence to grasp the complicated reasons behind what transpired in the adoption, a sense of abandonment settled into the recesses of my heart. And because it happened at such an early age, I scarcely knew any other way; it felt normal. Even into high school, there was a certain desperation in my efforts to be accepted. It was burned into the makeup of who I was as a child. Acceptance was extremely important.

This led to being bullied. Because I was so eager to be accepted, it was easy to take advantage of me and bully me. Here's an example that actually has a good ending. My best friend from school actually started out being a bully. He came to our school in fourth grade. One day he needed fifty cents to get some candy, and I gave it to him, trying to be winsome. Then the next day it happened again. Then the next. And the next. Soon I found myself in a relationship where I was giving him money almost every day and when I didn't have it, he would threaten to beat me up. This went on every school year until eighth grade. Finally, I was sick of the threats, and I told him I was through. He was stronger than me, but I didn't care. I didn't care if I lost the fight, I wasn't going to give him another red cent. This went down on a school bus on the way back from a basketball game and people were watching our little confrontation.

Can I be honest with you and say that was the most frightening three-hour bus trip I ever had in my life? People were expecting me to lose the fight. I was expecting to lose the fight. But I didn't care. I was just hoping that he would have a change of heart. The tension was thick. I could feel his eyes drilling into the back of my skull. I sat there for almost an hour kind of sweating, trying to come up with some plan in my head for how to pull off an upset. Then I saw a hand reach out to me. It was him, and he wasn't asking for money. He was offering me friendship.

The most relief I had ever experienced to that point in my life came rushing over me. See, all I wanted was to be friends with this guy. That's why I gave him fifty cents that first time back in fourth grade. Four years and a chunk of change later, it all came to a head. I could have refused him, and kept my grudge. For a brief moment, I considered it. But for some reason, I stretched out my hand and embraced him, and he remains one of my best friends to this day.

I wish they had all turned out that way.

There was one guy in the Scriptures that was bullied. His brothers bullied him, and they did horrible things to him. Joseph was the eleventh son of Israel (Jacob). The Bible teaches that Joseph was Israel's favorite son because he was the son of his old age (Genesis 37:3). Israel even gave Joseph gifts that he didn't give to his other sons. If you remember your colorful flannel board lessons from Sunday school, you'll recall that Israel gave Joseph a robe of many colors. All of this favoritism led to this:

> But when his brothers saw that their father loved him more than all his brothers, they hated him and could not speak peacefully to him. (Genesis 37:4)

bullied

Joseph did not ask to be the favorite. He didn't choose to be the son of Israel's old age. He just was. Neither did he ask for all of his father's special affection. He didn't ask for a robe of many colors, it was a spontaneous gift from his father. Imagine his growing frustration as he grew up. Ten older brothers, each of them gradually became more belligerent as they grew up together. As Israel poured out favoritism upon Joseph, his ten elder brothers became more and more disgusted. Finally when Joseph was seventeen years old, it had gotten to a point where none of his brothers would speak kindly to him.

I've been there. My experience with being bullied had little to do with favoritism, although there were some who accused me of being the teacher's pet (which was sometimes true). But I can relate to unrelenting ridicule. One day I forgot my notebook in one of my classes. The first hour I was able to go get it, I did. When I opened the notebook, I found a drawing of an extended middle finger with the words, "We don't like you. We don't care what you say." I have no idea who wrote that. It didn't matter. It was just another day in my life. When so many people have expressed their dislike, whom do you fight? You can't fight everyone. The only thing you can do is hope that tomorrow someone will give you a chance. At least that's where my logic had led me.

At this point, I should add a caveat to this story. The desire to find acceptance led me to be fairly goofy and annoying at many points in my childhood. Add to that a certain naivety that I possessed about people, the bottom line is that some of the taunting was earned. My junior year, at the prom, during one of the speeches given, I was told very publicly that people weren't laughing with me, but they were laughing at me and to get a life. Fortunately at this point in my life, I had been saved and was beginning to see things a little clearer. But that still hurt.

I sense that same kind of need for acceptance and naivety at work in Joseph. In Genesis 37:5-11, Joseph begins to share his dreams with the rest of the family. His dreams were lofty, and perhaps unknown to him at the time, prophetic. As one who was persecuted so heavily as a child, it is easy for me to recognize Joseph's desire to find acceptance in this. Something good was given to him. Something important was being said through his dreams. He shared those dreams with the hopes that his brothers would finally see that he didn't deserve the ridicule, which they so faithfully gave him on a daily basis.

Bullies are seldom ready to hear something good from the people they bully. Joseph's brothers were only infuriated by his dreams. Mainly because both of Joseph's dreams poetically describe how the entire house of Israel – mom, dad, and all the brothers – would be bowing down to him. This is where I think the naivety came into play. Maybe these aren't the best dreams to share with brothers who already despise you. Even Joseph's father, Israel, became offended at his dreams.

The dreams were the last straw. One day the brothers saw Joseph coming.

> They said to one another, "Here comes this dreamer. Come now, let us kill him and throw him into one of the pits. Then we will say that a fierce animal has devoured him, and we will see what will become of his dreams." (Genesis 37:19-20 ESV)

Fortunately, the oldest brother, Reuben, intervened and kept them from killing him. Instead they trapped him in one of the pits and Judah had him sold him into slavery. And from here the grand story of Joseph begins to unfold. From this moment we begin to really see what made up his character. When the pressure of life begins to squeeze you, your true character comes out.

I wish I could say that what came out of me while I was being bullied was as noble as what we see come out of Joseph. Ten years of ever increasing taunting, unkind jokes, and heartless rejection had really done a transformative work on me. Suffice it to say that I was angry, I was distrusting, I was desperate, and I felt like nothing was ever going to change my lot in life. But this was also all before I met Jesus.

What difference does Jesus make? That's a huge question. I'm not sure I can give you a complete answer because he's still making the difference in my life, even today! The experiences of my childhood have gone with me, every step of the way in my life with Jesus. As of this month, April of 2015, I have been born again for twenty-two years and eleven months. You'd think in that length of time a person would get over what was done. In many ways I have, thanks to the power of God. However, in small ways, those wounds still influence and exert power in my thinking. When you spend most of your childhood longing for acceptance, even when God comes in and makes you new, that old way of thinking can still hold incredible sway.

Joseph is an excellent model for showing us the difference that God makes when life has gone to hell. He suffered what you might characterize as an ultimate betrayal. The brothers who were supposed to love him, turned their backs on him, sold him into slavery, then lied to Israel by saying that wild animals had killed him. Not only did they abandon him, but they also destroyed any hope that anyone might go looking for him. Clearly, few of us suffer this severely, but this is precisely why Joseph can help us understand how God can help us endure our own much less severe trials. If God can make a difference under such extreme circumstances, surely he can help me!

Understanding one fact about God can make all the difference. God's acceptance is enough. If Christ has indeed saved you, there is nothing further you must do to be accepted by God. When we looked at adoption, one thing became clear. It is complete, it is permanent, and nothing will ever undo it!

> Who shall separate us from the love of Christ? Shall tribulation, or distress, or persecution, or famine, or nakedness, or danger, or sword? As it is written,

> "For your sake we are being killed all the day long;
> we are regarded as sheep to be slaughtered."
> No, in all these things we are more than conquerors through him who loved us. (Romans 8:35-37 ESV)

Oh that I would've grasped this early in my walk with Christ! What a difference it has made in me since I have allowed this truth to settle deep into my soul!

I believe we can see this same thing at work in Joseph. A seventeen-year-old kid, rejected, sold down the river by his siblings, and enslaved by a foreigner. Look at what happens in Potiphar's house.

> The LORD was with Joseph, and he became a successful man, and he was in the house of his Egyptian master. His master saw that the LORD was with him and that the LORD caused all that he did to succeed in his hands. So Joseph found favor in his sight and attended him, and he made him overseer of his house and put him in charge of all that he had. (Genesis 39:2-4 ESV)

God was with Joseph. Though the narrative shows that God never spoke directly to Joseph like he had spoken with Abraham, Isaac, and Jacob, it was clear that God was prospering everything that Joseph did.

How did Joseph go from outcast teenage brother to successful man? While it doesn't say it outright, the implication is that he had learned to trust God completely. Somewhere between the pit his brothers threw him in and Potiphar's house, Joseph realized that God's acceptance was the only acceptance he needed to worry about. He knew that to be accepted by God would mean to walk safely through any and every trial that this world would throw at him. He could work confidently for a man who could have him killed for even the smallest mistake because he knew that God had accepted him and was with him.

God's acceptance is the thing that frees us from needing the approval of people. When I began to understand that all of the approval, all of the acceptance I had ever craved had already been given to me through Christ, I began to let go of the need to fit in. For many years, I thought that the best life I could have would be found in a community of people who accepted me for who I was. That sounds right, and I chased it for most of my youth and young adult years. Even after being born again, I chased this kind of acceptance, just in different groups of people. I went from trying to be cool at school to cool at church. But I had it wrong. And as I began to realize this, questions arose in my heart. If God made us for community, why am I feeling empty even though I was drowning in church community?

When my wife met me, she called me *Mr. Church*. That's how integrated into the church culture I had become. Any church thing or fad that happened in the mid-to-late

1990s and early 2000s, I probably at least tried to latch on to it. Cheesy t-shirts? Check. Drama ministry? Check. Puppets? I tried. Bible drill? Check. Left Behind? Own the movie. WWJD? No bracelets, but in college I heard it ad nauseam. To this day, my brother-in-law, Casey, still mocks me for my religiosity. One time, he and I had to go get ice for a family get-together. The closest place was a liquor store, so he decided to go there for ice. According to him, I acted like it was a stealth black op where we needed to get in and get out without being seen as quickly as possible; make the money drop, take the goods, and get out!

God's patience with me is amazing. And what makes it more amazing is even in the midst of me choking on church, he was storing up things that would work out for my transformation later. By early 2007 I had reached a point where I was desperate. I was doing so much church stuff, but feeling so empty. I was actually on staff at our church as the worship leader and adult discipleship leader. I was doing all of this good stuff, but I felt spiritually anorexic.

I don't remember what led me to this, but that year I began to read through the Scriptures verse by verse and journal my thoughts. I began reading Christian books from authors whose works had stood the test of time. This was new for me. I had never been a person to keep a journal. I had never been an avid reader, especially of old books. Gradually, through these disciplines I began to emerge from my spiritual anorexia. And it began to sink in: I've been looking for acceptance in the things of God, not in God himself. How do I receive God's acceptance? Certainly not through more stuff!

> For all the promises of God find their Yes in him. That is why it is through him that we utter our Amen to God for his glory. And it is God who establishes us with you in Christ, and has anointed us, and who has also put his seal on us and given us his Spirit in our hearts as a guarantee. (2 Corinthians 1:20-22 ESV)

Adoption means acceptance. If God's promise includes my adoption when I trust Christ for salvation by faith alone, then full acceptance from God is part and parcel of the promise. And the good news is I don't do anything to earn more and I can't do anything to receive less. *It is God who establishes us with you in Christ . . . and who has put his seal on us and given us his Spirit.* In other words, God makes me acceptable! My zeal, my efforts, they have nothing to do with my level of acceptability before God! My acceptance relies completely upon his amazing grace, mercy, and affection toward me! How liberating! How unbelievable! This truth is at the same time the most freeing truth and the most hard to believe truth. I submit to you that it is harder to believe, even than the resurrection of Christ! Skeptics the world over may reject the resurrection, but believers the world over who wholeheartedly believe in the resurrection wrestle to believe that they are completely accepted and loved by God! And the truth is that I wrestle with it on a regular basis. But it's also true that I wrestle with it way less than I used to!

Look again to Joseph. A sure sign that you are allowing the truth of God's complete acceptance is when difficult times come, you are not shaken or surprised that they've come. Your faith and trust in the Lord remains steady. Some time after Potiphar put Joseph in charge of his household, Potiphar's wife took a liking to him because he was a good looking dude. She made advances at him, and one day caught him by his robe and demanded that he sleep with her. Joseph did the only thing he could do. He ran, and as he ran, his robe came off in her grip. He ran away essentially naked. Potiphar's wife, stung by the rejection, took this as an opportunity to frame Joseph for attempted rape. Potiphar believed his wife, because she had his robe, and threw Joseph in prison.

Talk about a bad day! But, Joseph's faith in God was not shook. Joseph knew he had been accepted and loved by God, and this gave him the confidence he needed to survive such a bad day! Many people would start turning inward, looking for a reason that God had abandoned them to prison. And here is one of the problems with many people's faith: it is horribly circumstantial. We equate good circumstances with God's favor, and bad circumstances with God's displeasure. Not Joseph.

> And Joseph's master took him and put him into the prison, the place where the king's prisoners were confined, and he was there in prison. But the LORD was

with Joseph and showed him steadfast love and gave him favor in the sight of the keeper of the prison. And the keeper of the prison put Joseph in charge of all the prisoners who were in the prison. Whatever was done there, he was the one who did it. The keeper of the prison paid no attention to anything that was in Joseph's charge, because the LORD was with him. And whatever he did, the LORD made it succeed. (Genesis 39:20-23 ESV)

Joseph's life was blessed at home. His life was blessed in slavery. His life was blessed in prison. It seems that no matter the circumstance Joseph found himself in, he was prospering and experiencing the love of God. Was it because of what he was doing? Not likely. Everything he did was getting himself into trouble with people. A blessed life has less to do with what you do and more to do with what you believe. Start with belief, and what you do will follow. If you believe you are completely accepted by God, in Christ, then your actions will show it. Your countenance will reflect it. Your love for others will demonstrate it. It is clear to me that Joseph had an incredible grasp on this precious truth. He isn't alone.

Peter, Paul and countless Christians throughout history, found themselves in prison for loving Jesus. And while prison wasn't the most enjoyable place, their faith was never shaken, and their hope was never quenched. What emboldened them? What maintained their disposition under trial?

Did they see their misfortune as being abandoned by God? Did they view their circumstance as God's displeasure? Not at all! Instead, because they knew that their circumstances had no bearing on God's love and acceptance for them, they could keep living for him and hoping in him no matter where they found themselves!

Fast-forward a bit. Joseph faithfully loved God during his time in prison, and God prospered him. In fact, Joseph was such a man of integrity, he was respected within the prison and eventually put in charge of all the prisoners. While in prison, God gave him an interpretation for a couple of Pharaoh's dreams. Successfully interpreting those dreams landed him the job of Governor of Egypt. As Governor, Joseph was responsible for the rationing of grain to the public. When famine hit, it drew in peoples from the surrounding nations seeking to purchase grain from the storehouses of Egypt. One day Joseph's brothers arrived looking for grain. After some elaborate testing of his brothers, Joseph can no longer contain himself.

> Then Joseph could not control himself before all those who stood by him. He cried, "Make everyone go out from me." So no one stayed with him when Joseph made himself known to his brothers. And he wept aloud, so that the Egyptians heard it, and the household of Pharaoh heard it . . . So Joseph said to his brothers, "Come near to me, please." And they came near. And he said, "I am your brother, Joseph, whom

you sold into Egypt. And now do not be distressed or angry with yourselves because you sold me here, for God sent me before you to preserve life." (Genesis 45:1-2, 4-5 ESV)

Only a man who understands his standing with God could say what Joseph says here. Not only is there forgiveness, but there is perspective. His mercy towards his brothers flowed out of the richness of God's mercy in his life. The perspective he possessed about his trials emanated from his belief that God had never abandoned him, but instead was carefully establishing each step of his journey. He even trusted that God worked through his brothers' bullying and wickedness.

> As for you, you meant evil against me, but God meant it for good, to bring it about that many people should be kept alive, as they are today. (Genesis 50:20 ESV)

That leaves me with a choice. If by God's grace, Joseph, could forgive his brothers for their atrocities, can I forgive, by God's grace, the people who bullied and insulted me when I was a child? The answer has to be, with no doubts, *yes*! Is it a done deal for me? No, I have to forgive them again and again. I'm Facebook friends with a few of them and sometimes when I see their posts, or when I see their pictures, I'm reminded of the insults, and I have to forgive again. The good news is the Spirit of God has never failed to grant me the grace to forgive. All I have to do is choose to take those thoughts, those memories captive and bring them into submission to Christ. Can I see the good that God is working out through their wickedness? I get glimpses, but even if I can't see the whole picture, I know one day I will, and it will be a glorious picture of God's loving grace and acceptance in Christ.

You have a choice today. Have you been bullied? Have you wrestled with trying to find acceptance among your peers? Let me encourage you. The acceptance that will change and transform your life can only be found in Jesus Christ. Believing in him for salvation will grant you a place at the table of the King of Glory, change your fundamental being and status, and provide for you an inexhaustible source of acceptance and freedom. Acceptance from anyone else will be filled with conditions and work in order to keep it. Acceptance from God, in Christ, is completely his work, removing from you the burden of remaining in his grace. There you will find, not only his love and acceptance, but also the means to forgive the people in your life who have bullied you and taken advantage of you. He did it for Joseph. He's doing it for me. He can do it for you as well.

recreated

References

1. *Tommy Boy*. Dir. Peter Segal. Perf. Chris Farley, David Spade, Brian Dennehy. Paramount Pictures, 1995. Film.

saved

One of the earliest memories from my childhood is actually kind of odd. Not odd that it's weird, but just odd that of all the things that happened around me as a child, this has stuck with me through the years. It's kind of fuzzy, but nonetheless, it's still with me. The memory goes like this. I'm standing behind my dad's recliner, pretending it is a pulpit, pretending I am the preacher from our church. I'm pounding my fists on the *pulpit* and shouting, "You must have the Holy Spirit!" I was probably five years old at the time, and for some reason, instead of playing with my toys, I wanted to imitate our pastor, Brother Bob. (Maybe that was a prophetic moment in my life since now I'm an ordained minister.)

I was five years old and the preacher had already made an impression on me. That's all I remember. I don't actually have any memories of him preaching. The only memory I have of Brother Bob is my imitation of him. Apparently he was of the fiery sort of preacher. But back in the day, as preachers went in northeast Mississippi, those were the most favored kind: the preachers who preached the Word with passion and guts. If your church had one, you gathered a following. If you didn't, the music and potlucks better be amazing.

This was, and to a large extent still is, the culture. Mississippi was (and still is) in the heart of the Bible Belt. Most families I knew attended church. When you met someone new, one of the first things you would learn is where they attended church. Church attendance was almost a given. As I got older, it became clearer to me that it wasn't always the case, but still for the vast majority of people, church attendance was a staple in their life.

Today there are forty-three Southern Baptist Churches in Union County, Mississippi.[1] As I browsed the list, I noticed some churches I knew from the 80s and 90s are missing, but it is still quite large. Union County, Mississippi covers four hundred seventeen square miles.[2] That means there is approximately one Southern Baptist Church for every ten square miles. Consider that I haven't even counted all the other denominations of churches. Union County, along with every county in Mississippi, is saturated with churches! Church is a cultural staple. Even as the Church is losing its hold on the culture in many regions across our nation, it still has a firm grip across the Deep South.

Temple Baptist Church in Myrtle, Mississippi is where I cut my teeth with church. With the exception of maybe four years of my childhood, Temple is where I grew up. Temple is where I learned most of the great stories of the Bible on a bright, colorful flannelgraph. It's where I first attended Vacation Bible School and sat through my first Gospel singings. First potlucks, first revivals . . . first business meeting; Temple was a lot of *church firsts* because I was practically born there and our family was faithful to attend. As I mentioned earlier, my grandfather, King Callicutt, was there when the church was first formed back in the 1940s. We definitely have some family history at Temple.

Yes, there were many firsts, including my first baptism. You read me right: *first* baptism. And subsequently also my *third* baptism, but I'll get to that shortly. My earliest memories of Vacation Bible School were probably from when I was six years old because it was at that VBS that I first remember understanding the Gospel. Brother Richard Johnson was our pastor. He was young, had kids just a little older than me, and as best I can remember was drawing people to the church. If I remember correctly, it was under his leadership that Temple built a *Family Life Center*, which was directly across the road from the church. It had a fellowship hall, classrooms, and a basketball court. It was the first one like it in Myrtle. I was six, so I had a six-year-old understanding of things. Brother Richard was cool in my book because he built a gym for us to play in.

Brother Richard also led our VBS. We didn't have a children's minister or a youth pastor at the time, so he bore the honors. Aside from the Kool-Aid and cookies, the thing I remember clearest about that VBS was the baseball diamond.

recreated

One day during VBS, Brother Richard pulled out a drawing of a baseball diamond, from which he explained how to get *saved*. I wish it was clear enough in my memories to recite verbatim to you, but as best I can remember, first base was to admit you are a sinner, second base was to repent of your sins, third base was to believe that Jesus Christ died and was raised from the dead, and home base was Heaven. It was something like that. Simple enough for a child to understand.

As he explained each step, I listened. It made sense to me. When he finished, he asked us all to bow our heads. While our heads were bowed, he asked if anyone wanted to go to heaven, and of course I raised my hand. Then he asked the ones who raised their hands to meet him down front. On that note, I froze. I was horribly shy. I stood there until I felt my friend, Curtis, start moving toward the aisle. Seizing on Curtis' momentum, I followed Curtis to the front. Brother Richard led us in a prayer to ask Jesus into our hearts, and that was that. In the weeks that followed, I went through a workbook for new Christians that was called Survival Kit, and I received my first baptism after I completed the book.

And that was it. Saved! That is, at least as far as anyone could tell. *You're saved, now go out there act like you love Jesus!* And for a six-year-old, that comprised mainly of being nice to my friends, obeying my parents, *not* hitting my sisters, and answering questions in Sunday School. This happened during the summer after first grade.

Second, third, fourth, fifth, and sixth grades came and went. You know what happened during those years? Not just the bullying I mentioned earlier, but there was a slide toward wickedness. As I got older, the angrier I became from the bullying, the fouler my language would get. By the time I was in fourth grade, I was cussing like a sailor in certain company. When fifth grade rolled around, I was starting to look at pornography whenever I could get my hands on it. In sixth grade, I was lying to my parents regularly, especially about what I was eating and drinking (I was a childhood-diabetic) and about the music I was listening to (hardcore rap music, supplied by my friends).

But on the surface, I was a good kid, and a good church kid to boot. We continued to faithfully attend church throughout my childhood. As far as I know, my parents were none the wiser about my little issues, so nothing was ever really talked about or dealt with parentally. And if they had known, there would've been beatings first and questions later.

By the time seventh grade arrived, I was trying to change my image a little bit. I started combing my hair different and wearing more stylish clothes. All I wanted was girls! But I was so ill-equipped to catch one! I was socially awkward, puberty was raging, pimples were rampant, and on top of that, I had no idea how to even do this. In fifth grade, on a Halloween hayride, a girl from my class started kissing me on the neck. I wasn't ready for that so I really ticked her off the next day at school, wrecking any hope of her ever liking me again. In seventh grade, I regretted that. Never again would a girl come to me so easy. This is no joke, the only girlfriend I could get was in eighth grade, from another school (so she didn't really know me that well), and I was too immature in my thinking to keep her for more than a couple of months.

I was approaching a time in my life where I might've tried anything to get an attractive girl who would stay with me. But in seventh grade, in a church revival at New Oak Grove Baptist Church, I heard something that I had never heard before in my life. I learned about the unquenchable, never-ending, never-cooling, always dark, yet always burning fires of HELL! Can I remember the evangelist's name? No. All I remember is his impassioned preaching, his vivid illustrations, his thundering voice, and his imposing size. He told us how the worms never die; how they will forever eat away at us, yet never consume us! He told us how Judas and Pilate are still trying to wipe the blood of Jesus off of their hands as they cry out in agony from the flames! He described how Satan and his demons, in their own torment, lash out at the men and women who are there to torment them further! It was intense to say the least.

There I was, standing toward the back on the left side of the room, scared to death. I really hadn't given salvation much thought since I was baptized as a six-year-old. Now I'm twelve and that salvation I thought I received when I was six seemed pretty distant. Now I'm faced with this new reality of hell. Am I going there? I knew in my heart that many of the things I was doing were wrong. The preacher was talking about feeling conviction. I didn't until this moment. All

I knew for sure is that I didn't want to end up in such a horrible place. But like before when I was six, I couldn't move. I was still really shy. I was petrified in place, scared to go, but scared not to go at the same time. Finally I looked up and I saw pretty much all of my peers down front. Feeling emboldened, I joined them.

Instant relief! The evangelist came by and prayed over each of us and led us in a *sinner's prayer*. And like when I was six, that was that. Except that for me, this was a *second* salvation experience. And a couple of weeks later, at New Oak Grove Baptist Church, I was baptized for the *second* time.

Now that I had been sufficiently scared into heaven, I felt like life might start to turn out better for me. Eighth grade was ok. Next to my senior year, eighth grade was probably the most bully-free year I experienced between seventh and twelfth grade. Ninth grade and tenth grades, however, would prove to be the two worst years ever. Rejection upon rejection, insult upon insult; I was the butt of so many jokes, I stopped counting. And I was still using foul language, looking at pornography, becoming increasingly dishonest, plus more temptations that came with getting older and maturing.

By this time, I was in youth group and back at Temple Baptist Church. Youth group was not a great experience. I've often told my wife that the one place where I had the best chance of fitting in – youth group – was a fail. Don't misunderstand, I had friends in our youth group, but as a whole I simply never felt like a square peg in a square hole. We had great youth pastors and youth leaders who poured their lives into us. That isn't lost on me either. But it was the youth themselves who were driving me further and further away from God. I was a fairly intelligent kid, and what I saw and experienced during those first two years of youth group – ninth and tenth grades – was making me question faith altogether.

One event above all kind of epitomizes what was pushing me away. Temple was putting on this weekend event where we invited ministry teams from other churches in the county to come and preach, teach, sing, and essentially do a mini-revival over the course of a weekend for the church. The youth group had a slew of their own events that ran alongside the adult events. I attended this all weekend. Over the course of the weekend, I saw several of the students rededicated their lives to Christ, and maybe a few even got saved.

I believe it was Sunday afternoon; a fight between a few of the youth broke out on the church lawn. These were some of the same students that made decisions just the night before. Later that night, the guy who was preaching to the youth, basically called everyone out for being fake, which was appropriate. I walked away from that weekend discouraged. Then to top it off, I began hearing things through the grapevine about the personal lives some of the older students on the ministry team that served us. Things that weren't too Christian. I went from discouraged to distraught. I looked at my life and all I saw was hypocrisy. I looked at the lives of my peers and all I saw was hypocrisy. Even the students who tried to lead us were apparently full of hypocrisy. The questions in my mind were along the lines of, "Is Jesus even real?"

I was saved (finally) at the age of fifteen in May of 1992 at a crusade on the W.P Daniel High School football field in New Albany. The summer after my sophomore year had just begun. This was my *third* (and only real) salvation experience, and my *third* baptism followed a few weeks later at Temple. How do I know it was real? Because it was only after this experience that my life actually began to change. God's grace had found me at last and my life hasn't been the same since! I know it was real because when I went down that night at New Albany's football field to respond to the invitation, I thought I was good. I thought I had already settled all of this (even in the midst of all my doubts, I hadn't totally rejected faith). I know it was real because my counselor, Sheldon, wasn't content to just lead me in a *sinner's prayer*. He contended with me for forty-five minutes after everyone else was leaving and the chairs were getting packed up! I know it was real because when the light of Jesus finally broke through the darkness of my dungeon, Sheldon didn't even have to lead me in a prayer, I joyfully prayed immediately to receive Him and His forgiveness! I know it was real because immediately I wanted to tell my friends! None of this happened like that before. Before I just went about my business as usual. Business couldn't be usual anymore for me! Finally I was saved and forgiven!

Now, why am I telling you this long, potentially boring testimony? There's something at work beneath all of this.

I was a good church boy, outwardly obedient, but on the inside dying, becoming progressively more wicked. Yet, somehow I was convinced that I was ok with God because I had walked down to the front of a church service, prayed a prayer, followed a preacher's instructions, and been baptized . . . twice. I know many believers whose experience is similar to mine. Convinced of their salvation because of an experience, a prayer, a tradition, a decision, yet nothing in their lives was showing evidence of the Holy Spirit's transforming power. This is the story of many believers in the Bible Belt. Hear me: Bible Belt Christianity can send you straight to hell. When Church becomes so cultural, so institutional, salvation can be summed up in a list of behavior changes, rather than heart transformation. If you act according to the social norms for Christians in the Church saturated culture, you're good. Faith doesn't rest in Christ, but instead it rests on good behavior. This is classic faith by works, and it's seductive because you'll win the approval of other religious men and women quickly and mistake it for the approval of God.

The apostle Paul may be the most vivid case we can find in the Scripture of a man who was convinced of his own salvation before he met Jesus. In Paul's day, you could say that Israel was the Bible Belt of the Roman Empire. Paul grew up in a culture where if you were religious, you could rise in the cultural ranks. Paul says this of himself:

> "I am a Jew, born in Tarsus in Cilicia, but brought up in this city [Jerusalem], educated at the feet of Gamaliel according to the strict manner of the law of our fathers, being zealous for God as all of you are this day." (Acts 22:3 ESV)

Paul pursued God by being educated by Gamaliel, one of the most sought after teachers in Paul's day. He was trained in the "strict manner of the law" and grew in his zeal for God through strict obedience to the Old Testament law. When his education was complete, he joined the ranks of the Pharisees.

> "circumcised on the eighth day, of the people of Israel, of the tribe of Benjamin, a Hebrew of Hebrews; as to the law, a Pharisee;" (Philippians 3:5 ESV)

In terms of zeal and spirituality, for a Jew this was the ultimate. Pharisees had it together. They knew the Scriptures. They obeyed the law. They had the trust and respect of the people. Pharisees didn't actually gain a bum rap until John the Baptist and Jesus came along and turned their world upside-down! So Paul was pursuing God the only way he knew how. He became zealous about the law. He became zealous about the purity of God's people.

> "as to zeal, a persecutor of the church; as to righteousness under the law, blameless." (Philippians 3:6 ESV)

Persecuting the Church was the only natural response because in his mind it represented a heretical departure from the law and the traditions of the Jews. This was Paul's work for God – to eradicate the Church before their message led more men and women astray!

Paul thought he was doing well. He had done everything that tradition and culture expected from him as a godly Jew. His salvation was supposedly secured through his zeal for obedience. I can't tell you how familiar that feels. Even though I had doubts, I had based my salvation on what I had done to secure it. I believed the right things. I prayed the right things. I *outwardly* behaved they way people expected Christians to behave. But I was completely lost, and so was Paul.

In Romans chapter seven, Paul gives us some insight into what had begun to happen in his heart in the time leading up to his salvation on the road to Damascus.

> "Yet if it had not been for the law, I would not have known sin. For I would not have known what it is to covet if the law had not said, 'You shall not covet.' But sin, seizing an opportunity through the commandment, produced in me all kinds of covetousness." (Romans 7:7-8 ESV)

It's curious that Paul singles out the tenth commandment, "You shall not covet" as the one that tripped him up. Timothy

Keller points out that of all the commandments, coveting is the only one that is completely an attitude of the heart.[3] Paul could have outwardly followed every other commandment to perfection, but the tenth commandment presented a problem because it wasn't outward. It was entirely internal, and it ran wild in Paul's heart. The more he tried to not covet, the more opportunities his heart took to covet!

Follow me for a minute. When I was younger, even after I was born again, but still an infant in my faith, I was still very much deep into my works affecting my acceptance before God. If your works are tied to your acceptance, what happens when you fail? Despair! How do you then lift yourself out of despair? Work harder! Double your efforts! For me, it was to be at church every time I could, be active in every church activity, read the Bible more faithfully, help more old ladies across the street, you get the picture. What this ultimately led me to was a burn out in my spiritual life, where no matter what I did, I still felt spiritually dry and bankrupt. It wasn't until I began to detach my acceptance with God from my works that my spiritual life began to flourish.

Look at Paul's life. He's a zealous Pharisee, highly educated, incredibly intelligent, and deadly serious about obeying the Law to perfection. And he was succeeding, except for that one final commandment. You shall not covet. What was the answer? More zeal, more activity, more study, more indignation, more dedication to loving the Law. And with each covetous failure the intensity increases because if you believe your works secure your acceptance, there is no other course of action.

Then one day a man named Stephen was brought before the Pharisees; a man who loved Jesus and was filled with the Holy Spirit (see Acts 6:8 – 8:3). Paul (then Saul) was on the council. They listened to his testimony about Jesus. They heard Stephen's prophetic, Spirit-filled, word to the council as he accused them of murdering the very Messiah whom they had been waiting for. He rushed Stephen, along with the rest of the council, covering his ears and screaming so he couldn't hear his message as they took him outside the city and stoned him. And from there, Paul was given permission to round up and imprison any Christian he could find.

Do you see the pattern? As a Pharisee, Paul's understanding of salvation, that works secure your acceptance with God, drove him to ever increasing levels of zeal, activity, and indignation at other people's sin, so much so that it led him to murder. I've never actually murdered anyone, but this pattern of failure and trying harder over and over again, each time putting a little more zeal in my efforts is so familiar. Bible Belt Christianity can work you to death.

Because the culture I grew up in was so religious, to feel saved you have to do a lot of work. You had to faithfully attend church, Sunday morning, Sunday night, and Wednesday night. You have to go to youth group and as many youth activities as you can. You have to do Bible drill. You have to attend Vacation Bible School. If you can sing, you should sing specials. Do you get it? These were the unspoken expectations that Bible Belt Christians chased after in order to feel like they're actually growing Christians. In some ways, these unspoken expectations are still alive and well. The danger implicit in these expectations is that anyone can do them, saved or unsaved. This is where I was drowning. I was an unsaved teenager, trying to fulfill all of these expectations that people had of Christians. I was being a *good boy* because I thought that's what Christians were supposed to do. And I for sure didn't want to go to hell, so I tried hard; and when I failed, I tried harder. So this cycle was perpetuating in my life, slowly killing me inside, and I suppose, had Jesus not intervened, would have ultimately pushed me away from God altogether.

Paul was on a similar trajectory. He was on his way to *try harder* as he rode his donkey to Damascus. But thankfully, Jesus intervened.

> "Now as he went on his way, he approached Damascus, and suddenly a light from heaven shone around him. And falling to the ground he heard a voice saying to him, 'Saul, Saul, why are you persecuting me?' And he said, 'Who are you, Lord?' And he said, 'I am Jesus, whom you are persecuting. But rise and enter the city, and you will be told what you are to do.'" (Acts 9:3-6 ESV)

After this encounter, Paul was never the same again. This encounter made such a difference in his life he eventually changed his name from *Saul* to *Paul*. The transformation in Paul's life was dramatic because his zeal for God had a tectonic shift. As Paul matured in his faith, he went from righteousness by works, to righteousness by faith alone! Look at the difference Jesus made in this Pharisee's life! The man who lived by the law to the nth degree met Jesus and later penned these words:

> "For by works of the law no human being will be justified in his sight, since through the law comes knowledge of sin. But now the righteousness of God has been manifested apart from the law, although the Law and the Prophets bear witness to it—the righteousness of God through faith in Jesus Christ for all who believe. For there is no distinction: for all have sinned and fall short of the glory of God, and are justified by his grace as a gift, through the redemption that is in Christ Jesus," (Romans 3:20-24 ESV)

Saul, the Pharisee, would have never spoken these words. For Saul, the works of the law were his only hope. But Paul, the man who met Jesus, had his world turned on its head. Works of the law, the expectations of the religious culture, those things no longer held sway. Acceptance from God depended solely on faith.

This is my testimony. I have spent most of my adult life trying to shake off the vestiges of Bible Belt Christianity. Even after being saved, it took me a long time to understand that my acceptance with God was based entirely Christ's work on the cross, and not on my performance as a Christian. My performance wavers constantly. I'm still too affected by sin to even say that my performance is mediocre. That's why it's important to get it in my heart that God has accepted me completely because of Jesus Christ, not because I'm performing well.

> "but God shows his love for us in that while we were still sinners, Christ died for us." (Romans 5:8 ESV)

The beauty in this verse is that God saved me, adopted me, accepted me while I was still sinning and knowing that I would continue to sin. Have you come to terms with this? Do you still evaluate your acceptance with God by your works; by how well you perform? Living that way looks great on the outside, but inside you're dying, starving for spiritual nourishment, longing for the affection of your Father. Here's the secret. When you stop working for affection, and realize that God's affection for you isn't conditional on your works, you will experience the freedom that Jesus spoke of when he said his burden is easy and his yoke is light. And for the first time, you will work for God out of an abundance of joy and gratitude and gladness of heart. When you work from that position, you will be like the person from Isaiah 40:31 who will *mount up on wings like eagles, you will run and not grow weary or faint*. You will truly love the Lord with no strings attached because of his great love for you in Jesus Christ. Your faith becomes an anchor of stability and your witness becomes a bright light in a dark world. I pray that today you experience this freedom. I am still discovering it every day. I don't think I will ever stop finding areas of my life where I have depended on works to be accepted. But I can tell you this: I am freer today than ever, and if I am faithful to repent, more freedom awaits in my future.

References
1. Union County Baptist Association, 2015. http://www.unioncountybaptist.com/UnionCountyBaptistChurches
2. United States Census Bureau, 2015. http://quickfacts.census.gov/qfd/states/28/28145.html
3. Timothy Keller, *Romans 1-7 for You*, The Good Book Company, Purcellville, VA, 2014.

forgiveness

As I sit here, trying to start my thoughts on this chapter, I'm listening to the band *The Brilliance*. They are my go-to music for putting my mind in a contemplative writing mood. The song playing this moment is called *Brother*.[1] The lyric goes like this.

> When I look into the face
> Of my enemy
> I see my
> Brother.
>
> Forgiveness is the garment
> Of our courage;
> The power to make the peace
> We long to know.

I've been tryin' to get down to the heart of the matter.[2] Don Henley was on to something. *Forgiveness, even if you don't love me anymore.* Forgiveness is often the elephant in the room. I can't tell you how many people I've sat down with, and after a short talk discover that the crux of their problems is a lack of forgiveness. To their surprise, many times the lack of forgiveness isn't actually stemming from their current issue, but stems from something earlier and has affected everything ever since. Forgiveness is crucial for human flourishing.

Think about it. If we lived in a world where there was no forgiveness, cold, merciless justice would decide everything. If there were no forgiveness, road rage would increase a thousand fold. If there were no forgiveness, vengeance would be the order of the day for all of us. Something as simple as a conversational interruption could spark a fistfight. Civility would be unknown. We would all descend into an almost tribal, gang-like existence where even the smallest wrong is met with brutal justice.

While you may think this isn't a far stretch for some areas of the world, think a little further, a little deeper. Many of those places that flashed through your mind are places where the Gospel has no light. Where the gospel of Jesus Christ has been shut out you see brutality and merciless vengeance in full force. The gospel of Jesus Christ is founded on God's heart to forgive. Jesus Christ, the only begotten Son of God, descended to the earth, was born to the virgin Mary, lived a sinless life in thought, word, and deed, and died the death that you and I deserve by shedding his blood on the cross so that God could *forgive* sinners.

To be a Christian is to be forgiven *and* to be a forgiver. Little did I know, but this reality was about to land on me like the proverbial metric ton of bricks (metric is heavier). When I was (finally) saved, there was kind of a honeymoon period with Jesus, where everything was new, where I was so happy about salvation, where it seemed that the mountaintop was endless. However, after a short while, the Holy Spirit began to nudge me about some things. One particular area was forgiveness. After all the bullying I had experienced over the years, there was considerable hatred in my heart toward certain people. My response? No problem! Forgiven! And I went my merry way. Or, so I thought.

Forgiveness is a deep work. It is never a blanket action. What I tried to do when I initially forgave is allow one moment of zeal to cover years of damage. Though my first response was genuine, what I gradually discovered was my understanding of how deeply I was hurt wasn't even close to on target. Years of bullying, years of jokes, years of being walked on plowed a deep and wide rift in my heart. It had been there so long, I knew no other way. I had no idea what it meant to be accepted. Shy, defensive, worried about what others think, I had erected barriers around this rift to keep me from falling in, and they were simply a part of who I was. They were *normal*. Jesus entered in and began to tear down those barriers and mend the rift. Not all at once, and not too quickly, but he has been methodical and patient as he mends me. With each barrier removed, I had to forgive all over again.

Here's one of those barriers. Because I had been bullied so often, my confidence was shattered. I had very little faith in my ability to succeed at anything. Upon meeting Jesus, that confidence received a gigantic boost because I truly began to take to heart the verse, *"I can do all things through him who strengthens me."* (Philippians 4:13) But with each challenge, I felt that fear creep into my heart. I still feel it today. Today, I know how to deal with it. Back then, I wasn't so sure. Back then when that fear crept in it immediately stirred up those old feelings of hatred. *If only they had left me alone!* In those moments I was more prone to go Old Testament on them and pray, *"God smite my enemy!"* (I was reading the King James Bible at that time) than to pray, *"God I forgive them as you have forgiven me."*

However, slowly, patiently, as the years have passed the Holy Spirit has taught me that forgiveness is much, much more a disposition of the heart than it is an action. That initial *action* that I took to forgive was noble, and was the right thing to do. But my actions were outpacing my understanding. I said, *"I forgive you,"* out of my fresh zeal for Jesus, not from the disposition of my heart. The transformation of my heart has been a much lengthier process. Today when I am confronted with those old feelings, the disposition of my heart is more transformed and forgiveness is offered more freely, more deeply, and with a greater sense of gratitude to Christ.

forgiveness

I wish I could tell you that I had some incredible *Aha!* moment. I wish I could tell you that one day in a brilliant moment of revelation I understood everything and those chains that dulled my confidence simply fell off. For most of us it doesn't happen that way. Learning to forgive as we have been forgiven is a revelatory process. Or to borrow the metaphor from Shrek, it's an onion thing. Each layer gets peeled back revealing a new layer. With each new layer, there's a fresh smell of the hurt, fresh tears to be shed, and forgiveness to be offered once again. And as the Holy Spirit shapes and molds you into a forgiving person, at least in my experience, the tears come less, and in their place a joy begins to rise.

Joy? How can tears from hurt be replaced with joy? Let me tell you plainly, I can't explain how. I only know that as I have allowed Jesus to increasingly become my source of joy and happiness in life, I increasingly take joy in forgiving people. Maybe that's because it was God's joy to forgive us in Christ. Remember the father's response to the Prodigal Son?

> But the father said to his servants, 'Bring quickly the best robe, and put it on him, and put a ring on his hand, and shoes on his feet. And bring the fattened calf and kill it, and let us eat and celebrate. For this my son was dead, and is alive again; he was lost, and is found.' And they began to celebrate. (Luke 15:22-24 ESV)

There isn't a hint of anger. There isn't a hint of regret. The father didn't look at his son and say *I'm not sure you deserve forgiveness.* He didn't remind his son of how deeply he was hurt. He didn't do the passive aggressive reminder thing and say *hey you spent all of the inheritance, you wasted it on hookers, gambling, and booze, and even though you don't deserve it, I forgive you.* The son came to his father a broken man, and the father didn't even let him finish his apology; he embraced him and immediately cranked up the celebration!

That's not what we do. Too many of us tag on an added dose of guilt to our forgiveness. Many of us are the passive aggressive type. I should know because I'm guilty of this. Someone asks for forgiveness, but before you offer it, you have to make sure they know what they're apologizing for so you slip the dirty laundry list into your monologue. Newsflash: they know what they're apologizing for, that's why they've come to you. And even if it wasn't the apology you were hoping for, if they're repentant, accept it. God does that *all the time* for us. Forgive as you have been forgiven.

Or maybe this is you. You're not passive aggressive, you're just passive. You offer forgiveness, but stop short of reconciling the relationship. It's easier to forgive, forget, and move on than to do the work of reconciliation. In essence, you forgive, but you don't rebuild. You just leave things the way they are and move on with life. That isn't genuine forgiveness. Let me explain.

One of the most misunderstood teachings of Jesus is *turn the other cheek.* The reason we misunderstand is because we're Americans. We read it and think, *ok, if someone hits me, don't retaliate, turn the other cheek.* To be clear, it does mean that, but that's not all it means. To a first-century middle-eastern individual, the cheeks are offered as a sign of relationship. When two friends greeted one another, they would exchange kisses on each cheek. So to strike someone on the cheek was to insult the relationship being offered. Therefore, to turn the other cheek after being struck on one cheek wasn't merely resisting retaliation. It symbolized forgiveness and a hope that the relationship could be reconciled. The fact that you offer it means that you still hope for a kiss instead of fist and that you still hope for a better relationship. Real forgiveness hopes for and pursues reconciliation.

What is reconciliation? It means that you work to rebuild the relationship to a quality that is better than before. When God reconciles us to himself, he doesn't simply restore us back to the same innocence that Adam and Eve possessed before the Fall. He one-ups things. He reconciles us by making things *better* than they were. How is it better? Before the Fall, Adam and Eve may have been sinless, and they may have walked with God in the cool of the day, but he did not reside within them! Adam and Eve were not indwelt by the Holy Spirit, so when tempted, they only had their consciences to guide them.

Not so with us! In reconciling us God has made the relationship better by indwelling us with the Holy Spirit. Now we have his voice, his guidance, his power with us always to help us live holy lives and resist the temptations we face. That's way better! That's why Jesus told the disciples that it was better for him to go away so that he could send the Holy Spirit (John 16:7). J. D. Greear puts it well by saying, *"The Spirit inside you is better than Jesus beside you."* [3]

Forgiveness cannot be genuine if it neglects to reconcile. If you're too lazy to do the work of reconciliation, you're not truly forgiving people as you have been forgiven. Passive forgiveness is self-serving because it spares you the stresses of actually dealing with conflict and facing your own failures.

Finally, you might just be the aggressive type. Your forgiveness is white hot with a furor to deal with everything right now and if you can't then just forget it. You don't have any sensitivity to allowing God to peel away the onion at his own pace. You're driven by a desire to make things right quickly and not let the sun go down on your anger. But beneath the veneer of righteousness are other motives that are self-serving.

Sometimes aggressive types push through quickly because they're performing. When you're performing, the act can only be good for so long before it wears thin. This can only mean that they've been disingenuous from the start. Others push through because it's a religious work that will bring them a sense of peace when they lay their head down to sleep. Again, this is self-serving because you're ultimately only concerned about your own personal sense of peace rather than the spiritual health of everyone concerned.

The kind of forgiveness that God intends for us is the kind that is offered by the Prodigal Son's father. It comes out of the joy of your heart to forgive the person who wronged you. That kind of forgiveness is *supernatural*. Practically, how do we exercise supernatural forgiveness? I mean, if it's of a supernatural quality, isn't it a fair assumption that we don't naturally possess it? This isn't a trick question, but you may be surprised by the answer.

> His divine power has granted to us all things that pertain to life and godliness, through the knowledge of him who called us to his own glory and excellence, by which he has granted to us his precious and very great promises, so that through them you may become partakers of the divine nature, having escaped from the corruption that is in the world because of sinful desire. (2 Peter 1:3-4 ESV)

Christians are supernatural people! Not of our own making, but because of what God deposits with in us when we are born again! Peter explains in the opening sentences of his second letter that God has provided his children with every supernatural resource that we will need in order to live godly lives. That alone washes away every excuse, every justification, every argument that a person could possibly raise as a reason for their failure to live a godly life.

How can we access this supernatural power that God has deposited within us? He grants this power to us *through the knowledge of him who called us*. In other words, we learn how to wield the supernatural power that God has given us as we increase in our knowledge of Christ. As we learn of him by reading the Word, and as we learn of him through communing with him in relationship, we will become handier, more proficient with the power that God has poured into us. You will discern better. You will understand your choices with more clarity. You will know with greater certainty which paths are the ones you should take. All because you commune and fellowship with the Holy Spirit of God in prayer, meditation, and generally speaking, truly relating to him as the person of the Godhead who is always with you.

Through this you become what Peter calls *partakers of the divine nature.* This is how you forgive supernaturally. This is how offering forgiveness becomes a joyful thing. The more the divine nature of God has sway in your life, the more you can joyfully forgive like the Prodigal Son's father. But you only get there by realizing that you are no longer merely human. You, quite literally, are *superhuman* because of the Spirit of God who gives you access to God's divine nature! Do we boast in this? Of course not! We only boast in the death and resurrection of Christ! And as Christ does supernatural feats through us, he is the focus, the center, the reason for it all!

I'm sure I'm spooking some of you out right now. *I thought you were a Baptist boy!* My allegiance is to the Scripture, not a denomination's interpretation of the Scripture. The Scripture is *super* clear that every believer is *supernatural* because of the divine nature of God within us. The degrees to which we access this divine nature will vary with each believer. And I submit to all of us that the degree to which we

forgiveness

access the divine nature will be an issue of judgment and reward when we stand before Christ. We *must* begin to reckon ourselves as supernatural beings because of the Holy Spirit of God within us. If we continue to operate as *only* human, we'll *always* struggle with forgiveness and anything else commanded by the Word.

As I got deeper into writing this chapter, God hit me with something. Currently I'm Facebook friends with one of those guys who used to bully me. After all, it is Facebook, the place where you can be *friends* with people who hardly spoke a kind word to you when you were growing up. God said, "Offer him forgiveness." In that split second, every justification I could think of popped up. *I have forgiven him. I don't want to do this on Facebook, I'd rather do it in person. He probably hasn't thought of this in years.* So I tried to keep writing.

Silence.

Nothing came to me. It's like the well dried up. I had writer's block. This is what happens when we try to stiff-arm the Holy Spirit. As I have reflected on my life, and spoke with people about their lives, there seems to be a consistent pattern. The moment you stiff-arm, the airwaves go silent between you and the Lord. Jesus wants us to forgive, but we justify our reasons for not forgiving. *They don't deserve to be forgiven.* If you're only forgiving people who deserve it, then it isn't really forgiveness. If they deserve it, then you're obliged to offer it, which means it's more like a wage. By nature, forgiveness is a gift and can only be given to people who don't deserve it. It ceases to be forgiveness if it is deserved.

Ok, I'll do it.

I sent him a Facebook private message. I said that I'd rather do this in person, but that's not probable because we don't live close. I forgave him. I didn't present a long list of offenses, I just said you tormented me when we were younger, it affected me, and I forgive you. I told him I don't expect a response; I only needed to say this. If he never responds, it'll be ok because I was obedient to God and I said those things to him with great joy and hope in my heart. What will the result be? I have no idea. The results, in him and in me, are up to God.

> Forgiveness is the garment
> Of our courage;
> The power to make the peace
> We long to know.

Those lyrics aren't inspired Scripture, but I believe they reflect the right intent. If you're a believer, you can look in the mirror and see two different people. Many of us see a person who can't get things right. Always stumbling, always making the wrong choice, always giving into temptation; never praying enough, never sharing enough, never giving

forgiveness

enough. Falling prey to this version of ourselves happens for a lot of reasons. For me, and I suspect for many, we fall prey to this because we've bought the lies that people spoke into our hearts. But when you choose to put on the garment of forgiveness, courage begins to surge. Why? Forgiving the people who tore you down means that at some level you no longer believe they were correct. You slowly begin to see the other person in the mirror that has been saved by grace. Always forgiven, always loved, always protected; never condemned, never abandoned, never alone.

When you begin embracing the *new* self, when you daily purpose to wear a garment of forgiveness, courage rises. You begin to believe God for greater things. But embracing the new self is a daily choice. You have to fight the old self off in order to put on the new self.

> Do not lie to one another, seeing that you have put off the old self with its practices and have put on the new self, which is being renewed in knowledge after the image of its creator. (Colossians 3:9-10 ESV)

The new self is being renewed and transformed into the image of our creator! The more you wear the new self, the more you will forgive! The more you forgive, the more it becomes a joy because you know that God has forgiven you for so much more! This is where you cross from being merely human to supernatural because the new self is empowered by the Spirit of God; the same power that raised Christ from the dead!

Before I wrap up this chapter, I said earlier that being a Christian is to be a forgiver *and* forgiven. The supernatural forgiveness that all Christians possess is rooted in the reality that all Christians have been forgiven. It is impossible for anyone to forgive supernaturally unless they have been supernaturally forgiven. Christ paid for our forgiveness on the cross. I would still be harboring my anger and bitterness – and who knows what kind of man I would have become – if I had not experienced the forgiveness of God in Christ. I've said several times that we are to forgive as we have been forgiven. Here's why:

> Be kind to one another, tenderhearted, forgiving one another, *as God in Christ forgave you*. (Ephesians 4:32 ESV)

This naturally leads to the question, *how has God forgiven us?* First, as the verse tells us, he forgave us *in Christ*. That simply means the only way you can receive forgiveness from God is through Jesus Christ. There are a lot of religious guys who have tried to attain God's forgiveness through their own efforts and merit. God has clearly shown us that our merit, our works, can never earn his forgiveness. Like we said earlier, forgiveness can never be earned because if it were, it wouldn't really be forgiveness. It's like this: if you paid your last car payment to your bank, and then the bank president met you at the door as you were leaving and said, "Congratulations, we've forgiven your debt," it would make no sense. Forgiveness had no meaning because you had worked hard and paid off your debt on your own. God's forgiveness cannot be earned. No one's forgiveness can be earned. Forgiveness is a gift untied to merit, and God's forgiveness comes to us through Jesus Christ.

Christ is the means of God's forgiveness, but why do we need God's forgiveness? You may not realize this, but you and I are murderers. *Say what?* The reason Christ had to be crucified is because you and I are sinners. All of humanity is born spiritually dead in sin. The only way God could rescue the human race was to send his Son, Jesus, to die in our place. The answer to the age-old question, *who murdered Jesus,* is simple: We all did. We deserved to die for our sins. But Jesus, who never sinned, took our death sentence upon himself on the cross, and became the first man *ever* to die undeservingly. Then, because God is just, he raised Jesus from the dead (because he didn't deserve to die), gave him a body that can never again die, and gave him all authority in heaven and earth.

Anyone who believes this about Jesus and repents from their sins will receive God's forgiveness. And that forgiveness covers *all* of your sin, even the ones you haven't committed yet. How can this be? He promises that the good work he begins in you when he forgives you and saves you *will be completed* (Philippians 1:6)! That means that none of your future sins will thwart the ultimate work of God in your life to transform you into someone who looks like, talks like, acts like, loves like Jesus! Amen!

Do you see it? Can you see where the power for supernatural forgiveness comes from? A life forgiven by God is infused with grace that is abundant enough to cover your sins *and* spill over into the lives of everyone you touch! This is what King David meant when he penned the words, *you anoint my head with oil, my cup overflows* (Psalm 23:5). The grace given to you and I overflows because we've received *more than enough!* The Prodigal Son's father's forgiveness overflowed into his son's messed up, jacked up life. Christ is waiting for us to forgive like that. On the cross he paid for our ability to supernaturally forgive anyone and everyone, no matter the offense. I'm a totally different person because I choose to forgive with the power that has been given to me. With this kind of power at our disposal, the only person stopping you from forgiving is you.

References

1. David Gungor, Ian Croc, John Arndt, *Brother*, 2014, Brownie Hawkeye Music (Admin. by Capitol CMG Publishing). CCLI No. 7039054.
2. Don Henley, John Souther, Michael W. Campbell, Donald Hugh Henley, *The Heart of the Matter*, 1989, Sony/ATV Music Publishing LLC, Warner/Chappell Music, Inc.
3. J. D. Greear, *Jesus Continued . . . : Why the Spirit Inside You is Better Than Jesus Beside You*, 2014, Zondervan, Grand Rapids, MI.

people pleaser

There are a lot of Proverbs about friendship, which means there is a lot of wisdom involved in finding quality friends. One of the things that made me so easy to bully when I was younger is that I was desperate to be liked. I hated the thought that someone didn't like me. Unfortunately, my social skills were a bit later to bloom than many. I would make effort after effort to be friendly. I would try to joke. I would try to be likeable. But it often ended in failure. In fact, I had tried so hard, that I earned a mention in the senior class of 1993s will and testament to the junior class – my class: *Shane, understand that we are laughing at you, not with you.*

Wow. Even as I typed that, I felt a little hurt all over again. Look, the truth is, I did try way too hard. C. S. Lewis made a simple but crucial observation about friendship in his book, *The Four Loves*.

> Friendship is born at that moment when one man says to another: "What! You too? I thought that no one but myself . . ."[1]

Friendship is born on common interest. If you try to make friends by merely desiring friendship, you will fail. Friendship is discovered and forged when you discover someone with similar passions and beliefs. When you try to win friends through impressing, through trying to be as funny, through over-the-top niceness, you are laying a trap for yourself. You come off as a push-over who will do whatever you're asked. And when you refuse to do something, you get ridiculed because they know you won't fight back. When you're trying too hard to win friends, you essentially give everyone around you all the power in your life. That's what I did for years.

One term for this is *people pleasing*. You spend your life doing things for people, befriending, maybe suffering lots of rejection, maybe not, depending on your people skills. But no matter what the outcome, in every instance of people pleasing you give away all of your power and influence in the relationship in the hopes that you will be accepted. But all is not what it seems. The surprising truth about people pleasing is that under the surface, it has nothing to do with making other people happy. It's actually about making you happy. It's a self-serving method of trying to gain affection. You want the affection of particular people and if necessary you'll become a fool to obtain it.

people pleaser

You'd think that once a person meets Jesus, receives salvation, and is born again that this kind of behavior would cease. You'd think that God would uncover the dirty truth about your people pleasing ways right away. You'd think wrong. Or at least, in my case, if God did try to reveal it I wasn't paying attention. People pleasing was a blind spot in my life for many years after I was saved. And as my social skills improved (gradually), my people pleasing only became subtler and more sophisticated.

I've made no secret about the fact that I've been a church kid my whole life. The first and easiest place there was to please people was in church. After I was saved, I underwent some swift changes. I gained confidence. I lost my fear of speaking in front of people. My senior year, I discovered a love for singing. The church became a place where I could use these new talents and get some easy ego strokes. For what it's worth, I didn't see it that way, but in retrospect, I put a lot of my self-worth in my ability to perform. What does this have to do with people pleasing? Everything!

People pleasing is a means by which people try to feel worthy. My potential for making people happy through my gifts and talents had a direct correlation with how useful and valuable I felt. I had endured so much rejection in my growing up years, that when I finally started to feel the warm glow of acceptance from people, I craved it. I pursued it. It had me in it's grip and I didn't even know it. Acceptance had become my drug. To some degree, even today, I still feel its tug on my heart. I still hate rejection. I don't think anyone enjoys being rejected. The difference in me today and me back then is that God has worked to progressively transform my mind and my heart into someone who loves Jesus more than the acceptance of people. But that transformation has meant enduring some really hard relationship trials.

When I married Radene, I was still unaware of my people pleasing ways. It never occurred to me that my appetite for acceptance was actually a character flaw that would take us through a few of our most difficult trials. Don't take this the wrong way. In terms of conflict and difficulties, our marriage has been blessed if you compare it to many. However, that doesn't mean that the pain is any less potent. The trials we have endured have been difficult. My people pleasing made our relationship in the midst of those trials very tense. I came face to face with how deeply I was ruined by the desire for acceptance.

The first time I truly met this head on was after we had been married for about five years. I had been serving our church in the youth ministry and had been our church's worship leader for a year or so. I was so young and green in leadership. Our pastor had befriended me and taken me under his wing to train me in leadership. And I was soaking it up. He had a passion for Jesus that I wanted to mimic. He was a good preacher of the Word and I was learning more than I ever had before. On top of that, he affirmed me in my gifts. On the surface this was a good pairing. But for someone with my particular need for acceptance, this was ultimately poisonous for my character.

All the while, as I was being mentored, there was a lot of turmoil in the church that some were blaming on our pastor. This began to drive a wedge between me and Radene. She and I simply didn't see eye to eye on what was happening. To my shame, I was valuing my friendship with our pastor over my relationship with my wife (although I couldn't see that). He didn't know it, but he was encouraging me in ways that puffed me up. I was becoming arrogant. On one occasion, I shared with him some difficulties I was having with getting Radene on the same page, and his response, in so many words, was essentially, *you're the head, you're the husband, the buck stops with you*. I was so naïve and untrained in how to understand the Scripture, I would read Ephesians five and totally miss the point.

It all came to a head one day. I don't even really remember what the particular issue happened to be (and neither does Radene . . . whew!), but I confided something to our pastor, that inadvertently threw Radene under the proverbial bus. Let me stop here. Why would I throw my wife under the bus on purpose? That's just it: I wouldn't! But when you're constantly craving approval, your sense of up and down in your relationships can be terribly off course! It's a relational vertigo of sorts. You can betray trust and still believe you are doing the right thing. So the next thing I know, I received a call from her while I was at work saying that she was going to stay with her parents for a few days. This was the only day of my life where I left work for something other than having babies, sickness, death, or doctors. I rushed to my wife to make things right.

This was the first eye opener for me. My people pleasing was affecting my marriage. And it was the first time anyone had ever pointed out to me that I was a people pleaser. Of course I initially denied it, but as we worked things out, it gradually became clear to me. I had a problem, but I wasn't sure how to fix it. As I prayed and searched the Word on how to overcome this problem, God led me to take a look at the life of King Saul. Saul was a man whom God chose, but he gradually chose God less and less. Saul had every advantage given to him; he had absolutely no reason to be fearful or concerned about popular opinion. He was physically impressive; he was handsome (1 Samuel 9:2); at the beginning he even demonstrated a sense of meekness (1 Samuel 10:26-27). Yet he was still a people pleaser at heart.

The first recorded case of Saul's people pleasing ways is found in 1 Samuel chapter 13. Since God had given Saul success over the Philistines, the Philistines were understandably angry and ready for a *real* fight.

> And the Philistines mustered to fight with Israel, thirty thousand chariots and six thousand horsemen and troops like the sand on the seashore in multitude. They came up and encamped in Michmash, to the east of Beth-aven. (1 Samuel 13:5 ESV)

people pleaser

The sight of this struck fear into the hearts of Israel. So much that people were hiding themselves in tombs and wells for fear. At some point, maybe early on in Saul's reign, the prophet Samuel had given instructions to King Saul that before going to battle he should wait for his arrival to make sacrifices to God. Saul waited for seven days on Samuel to arrive. The people began to get restless, they were beginning to leave, fearing that Samuel would never come do the sacrifice, which would be a sign that God was not with them for this battle.

What's a people pleaser to do? Saul knows what Samuel has said, but Samuel has failed to show up in a *timely* manner. The people are deserting the camp for fear. Saul does what every people pleaser does. He takes the pragmatic approach. People pleasers are pragmatists when it comes to keeping the approval of their peers. Whichever course of action will assure that I am still accepted and loved will be the best approach.

> He waited seven days, the time appointed by Samuel. But Samuel did not come to Gilgal, and the people were scattering from him. So Saul said, "Bring the burnt offering here to me, and the peace offerings." And he offered the burnt offering. (1 Samuel 13:8-9 ESV)

The pragmatic solution isn't always the godly solution. Saul took matters into his own hands and offered the

recreated

sacrifice that Samuel was supposed to offer. In doing this, not only was he disobeying Samuel, but he was disobeying God. God wanted Saul to wait for his instruction and blessing through Samuel. But rather than please the Lord, Saul felt like pleasing the people would be more expedient and would keep the people from leaving. The consequences were beyond anything that Saul could have imagined.

> And Samuel said to Saul, "You have done foolishly. You have not kept the command of the LORD your God, with which he commanded you. For then the LORD would have established your kingdom over Israel forever. But now your kingdom shall not continue. The LORD has sought out a man after his own heart, and the LORD has commanded him to be prince over his people, because you have not kept what the LORD commanded you." (1 Samuel 13:13-14 ESV)

A single act of disobedience is all it took for Saul to alter his entire legacy, the future of his family. In all likelihood, this wasn't Saul's first act of people pleasing. However, this was probably the first one that really cost him. People pleasing always ends up costing you something. For me, it was ruining my relationship with my wife (and consequently God). Even though I was growing in a lot of ways by knowledge of the Word and in my understanding of leadership, I was growing out of order. I was shrinking in my primary ministry: the ministry to my family. For Saul, even though he was king, would become a smaller and smaller man, consumed by his desire to look good rather than actually being godly.

For the religious person, it's actually easy to confuse the two. I was religious. Saul was religious as well. Saul knew the rules. I knew the rules. Saul knew the jargon. I knew the jargon. Yet, we both were missing the boat. Both of us were set apart by God, Saul to be king, me to salvation, but we both seemed to miss the point. I was becoming the very thing that I never wanted to be. I was becoming a Pharisee. More concerned about the externals of faith than being changed on the inside. I knew that my primary ministry was my family (because that was the correct answer). But I was *functioning* as if the church was first. Saul knew that his first responsibility was to hear from God, but he *functioned* as if the people's voice was more important, and justified that behavior by the outcome.

> Samuel said, "What have you done?" And Saul said, "When I saw that the people were scattering from me, and that you did not come within the days appointed, and that the Philistines had mustered at Michmash, I said, 'Now the Philistines will come down against me at Gilgal, and I have not sought the favor of the LORD.' So I forced myself, and offered the burnt offering." (1 Samuel 13:11-12 ESV)

I was justifying my own behavior by the outcome as well. Up until that day the success of my ministry was measured by how many hands were raised in worship. How many shouts, how many tears, how many *thank you's*, these had all become barometers of success. And for the record, external expressions are one way to get an idea for your ministry's effectiveness, but definitely the least important one! But I allowed them to be my sole indicator because they made me feel successful. They gave me a sense of acceptance. Before this I thought Radene and I were doing pretty well. We had disagreements, but so does every married couple. Right?

I was judging my marriage on externals as well. We didn't argue like other couples. We didn't drag our problems out for a public airing like some couples do. We were attending church, and we were tithing. We were having people into our home, we had great friends, great extended family, and I had a stable job with reasonable pay. So, I allowed the calm exterior of the surface to sing me a lullaby. Therefore, the day I received that phone call, my world was turned on its head. What I thought was secure, was horribly insecure. What I believed to be healthy had fallen ill on the inside.

I'm sure Saul had begun to judge his kingdom on externals. Militarily he was successful. Politically, he was successful. While he knew that it was God who was granting him success, I suppose he began to assume that it would always be so. Scholars are unsure about how much time passed between Saul's anointing, and this foolish sacrifice that he presumed to make, but regardless of how much time elapsed it was enough for Saul to fall in love with his popularity more than his God. Being well-liked became his drive. You'd think that this event would've been enough to snap him out of it. He may have lost the kingdom, but he still had many years ahead to repent and still forge a godly legacy. Unfortunately, people pleasing has deep roots. For Saul, the rest of his life would be a struggle to love God more than the approval of men.

For me, Radene and I worked through this moment in our life. I realized how foolish I had been. I began battling this need for acceptance and approval. Honestly, I didn't even know how. Those were some of the most emotionally trying days of my life. I'm pretty sure it's when I started getting gray hair. I had days where I wanted to quit. I had days where I wanted to pack our family up and move away to a new place. But I was discerning enough that I knew those solutions were also foolish. I wish I could say that this difficult moment was the cure. Seldom is that the case with anything. That was the first chop at a thick, deep root. It was a big chop, but it wasn't the last.

A few years later, we found ourselves in a dispute between family members. Words were exchanged, feelings were hurt, and in the process of this, Radene was deeply wounded by some of the words that were lobbed in her direction. I had a role in the dispute as well, but unfortunately, a disproportionate volume of the criticism was getting laid upon my beloved. What's a recovering people pleasing husband to do? I slip immediately into fix-it mode. *What does the*

Bible say about conflict resolution? Let's do it! When can we meet to clear things up and get this over with? As soon as possible! The Bible says not to let the sun go down on your anger, so let's get on with it!

Some of you might admire my devotion to quickly practice what the Scripture teaches. You might be like I was, eager to resolve things (queue Morgan Freeman's voice) *expeditiously*! Beware if you feel as I did. For sure, there are kinds of anger that should be resolved quickly. Most of the spousal disagreements that Radene and I have endured have been the one-day kind, and the next day it is forgotten. But there are some wounds that get inflicted where the anger simply cannot subside before sunset. Blame it on a lack of faith, blame it on poor spiritual formation, but the bottom line is because none of us are fully transformed, all of us are still susceptible to hurts and wounds that don't go away quickly.

I wish that I had recognized this. Alas, I did not. Once again, I was being counseled to be the *head of my house* and take control of this situation. And oh my, how Scripture was being used to build a case for quick resolution. Matthew 5:9, Matthew 5:24, Matthew 18:15-17, Ephesians 4:26, and so on; I was on Bible overload for how to deal with this conflict. Plus, I already knew these verses, so I had already thought of these, but now they were being echoed back at me from others. And my people pleasing kicked in once again. I started suggesting to Radene that we need to resolve this as soon as possible. For me, that meant at least this week. For her, it meant something entirely different. What I felt like was gentle suggestion that we deal with this quickly, for her was insensitive to her hurts and wounds – insult on top of injury.

It was nearly three months before we sat down and resolved things. It was the longest three months of my life. I came face to face with my people pleasing once again. Am I more concerned with the perceptions of others, or am I more concerned with the health of my wife's emotional and spiritual life? Of course I am more concerned for my wife! Loving her by putting off my desire to fix things immediately was actually the most godly thing I could do for her. I may have ruined a few stress balls along the way, but it gave the Holy Spirit time to surface a few things. He brought things to light that needed attention that we might not have otherwise known about. I am pleased to say that after we reconciled with our family members, that relationship became better than it had ever been. The Lord is faithful to those who wait upon him. If I had asserted myself, the harm done to my relationship with Radene would have been deep and wide and who knows how that particular family relationship would have faired.

This brings me to one side point, simply because it has reared itself in both of my stories. Husbands, headship is not a position of *authority and decision making,* but rather it is a position of *service and responsibility.* Ephesians 5:25 instructs you to love your wives as Christ loved the church. How does he love the church? He serves her and protects her. As much as a wife is to submit to her husband, a husband *submits* to his wife's needs out of love, and both out of reverence for Christ

(Ephesians 5:21). If I had asserted myself and did what I wanted to do in that situation, it would've been a *violation* of my headship, not an *assertion* of it. Husbands assert their headship through servant leadership and shepherding, not through authoritarian leadership and demands.

In fact, King Saul didn't lead Israel through servant leadership. If you take Saul's reign as a whole, you will find that he was an authoritarian and did whatever worked to his advantage regardless of God's command. He didn't shepherd Israel. He didn't lead her through demonstrating a servant's heart. He started well, but as we saw, his people pleasing led to the kingdom being taken away from his family. He would continue to be king, but after him, another family would take his place. Unfortunately, that moment of judgment didn't lead him to genuine repentance. He continued in his folly. He almost killed his own son, Jonathan, over an ill-conceived vow (1 Samuel 14:24-46). Finally, there was one last act of people pleasing that ruined what remained of Saul's reign as king.

In 1 Samuel 15, God instructs Saul – through Samuel – that he is to attack Amalek, and spare no one, not even the livestock. Indeed, Saul did defeat Amalek, but he did what he thought was best rather than listen to the voice of the Lord.

> But Saul and the people spared Agag (king of Amalek) and the best of the sheep and of the oxen and of the fattened calves and the lambs, and all that was good,

> and would not utterly destroy them. All that was despised and worthless they devoted to destruction. (1 Samuel 15:9 ESV)

Saul had mercy upon Agag. Saul saw all of the good livestock and thought, what a waste! So he disobeyed the command of God for what seemed like a better plan. Let's not be too harsh on Saul, it does seem like a waste to kill perfectly good livestock. And why not demonstrate mercy to a fallen king? It might render future dividends from the remaining Amalekites to show their king mercy. I can honestly trace out the logic that was running through Saul's mind. The people were happy to get the fresh livestock, the Amalekites would be indebted to him for sparing Agag. What outcome could possibly be better?

We do this too. We second guess the command of God. Rather than simply obey the Lord, we justify that our plan would have better immediate results. Our plans would make us happier sooner. But . . . this is exactly the logic that led to the final dismissal of Saul as Israel's king. See God's response:

> And Samuel said to Saul, "I will not return with you. For you have rejected the word of the LORD, and the LORD has rejected you from being king over Israel." As Samuel turned to go away, Saul seized the skirt of his robe, and it tore. And Samuel said to him, "The LORD has torn the kingdom of Israel from you this

> day and has given it to a neighbor of yours, who is better than you. (1 Samuel 15:26-28 ESV)

While Saul did continue to reign as king, what the Scripture reveals is that shortly after this day, God commanded Samuel to go to the house of Jesse and anoint one of his sons, David, to be king.

> Then Samuel took the horn of oil and anointed him in the midst of his brothers. And the Spirit of the LORD rushed upon David from that day forward. And Samuel rose up and went to Ramah. (1 Samuel 16:13 ESV)

Saul continued to reign as king over Israel for fifteen years after David was anointed. But the Holy Spirit had departed from him and *rushed upon David from that day forward*. Saul only remained king because of the servant heart of David. If you continue reading the story, David enters Saul's service. The man who was truly king, anointed king, the rightful head of Israel, served the deposed king for fifteen years before actually taking the throne. David had two occasions where he could have killed Saul, and it quite literally would have been self-defense, for Saul was seeking to kill him. But he refused, not wishing to take matters into his own hands, waiting for the Lord to give him the kingdom, instead of taking it for himself. (See 1 Samuel 24 and 26)

David learned to lead through service by serving the man who wanted to kill him for fifteen long years. And to complicate the matter, David loved Saul. David married Saul's daughter, Michal (1 Samuel 18:17-30). Saul was David's father-in-law! David, perhaps more than anyone before Christ, learned to lead through serving, even those who hated him. David couldn't have done this by people pleasing. If he wanted to please the people in his life, he would have killed Saul the first time he had a chance to do so.

> And the men of David said to him, "Here is the day of which the LORD said to you, 'Behold, I will give your enemy into your hand, and you shall do to him as it shall seem good to you.'" (1 Samuel 24:4 ESV)

If the roles had been reversed, Saul would have taken his opportunity. David was not a people pleaser. Ultimately, we know that David had his own demons to wrestle with, but even when later his son Absalom led a coup and took the kingdom for a short while, he would not raise his hand to retake the throne by force, though his people thought he should. He knew his acceptance before God was the most important acceptance to enjoy.

People pleasing has never led any friend, any spouse, any leader to any real godliness. Acceptance is something that *every* person needs. We all have deep emotional and spiritual needs to be accepted. You must choose whose acceptance is most important. Will you be captive to the acceptance of peers that waver and change with every shift of the cultural wind, or will you be captivated by the acceptance of God, who never changes? In Jesus Christ, God accepts us as adopted sons! Understanding and believing this fact can change the course of your life! Are you a believer, but still trapped in people pleasing? Careful. You can never lose your salvation, but your saved life on this earth will be robbed of every ounce of joy, and your life in eternity will be robbed of many rewards.

Where am I in this journey? I'm still on it. The journey from people pleaser to God pleaser doesn't suddenly stop. In reality, all believers are on this same quest. Your mileage may vary, depending on your personality and disposition. But one thing I know for sure. As long as I pursue Jesus, I will be confronted with the same choice. Please people (including me) or please Jesus. If I ever find that I am in a place where I am not constantly faced with that challenge, I suspect that I will be dead and with my Jesus because living as a believer in a world that wants you to conform to its ways means there's a constant struggle over whom to please. As long as we remain in this flesh, we struggle to please God. We war. And that leads us to what's next.

References

1. C.S. Lewis. *The Four Loves.* Harcourt Brace & Company, Orlando, FL, reprinted 1991.

fight

I mentioned earlier that I hate conflict. I'm really not sure if anyone actually enjoys it. It raises your blood pressure, it surges your body with adrenaline and cortisol, the brain actually redirects blood flow away from your gut to your muscles, respiration increases; you become a physical wreck when you're angry. Look at Presidents Clinton, Bush, and Obama. They started with their normal hair color, but because of the daily conflict and stress of the job, they ended, or will end, with mostly gray or silver hair. If conflict has such an adverse effect on our bodies, it stands to reason that we should avoid conflict when possible. Right? Well, maybe and maybe not.

If you've trusted Jesus Christ for salvation, you'll find that conflict is the *natural* state of affairs for believers in this world. As much as we have been commanded to live peacefully with people (Romans 12:18), there are dimensions of the Christian life where, as long as we live in this world, there will never be peace. The conflict rages every day. For me, this has been the hardest part of growing and maturing in my faith. I despise conflict. As a recovering people pleaser, the path of least resistance is always a temptation. One of the things I have had to learn in my life is to embrace *the fight*. Warring against my personal demons, against my temptations, against apathy, against anything that would lead me away from my devotion to Jesus is an every-waking-hour endeavor. And it is tiring if you don't learn how to fight the right way.

I also told you in chapter two that I wasn't really a fighter. I'm positive that the whole thing about hating conflict played into that somehow. The few fights that I have been in, when I won I won by virtue of my size and strength not my fighting skills. My fighting skills were pretty much learned from the first four Rocky Balboa films, the first two Karate Kid films, and the world of professional wrestling. I did, in fact, attempt to pile drive someone in sixth grade . . . attempt. In the long run, those skills never proved reliable. Therefore, I never really felt like I was much of a fighter.

If fighting spiritually were anything like World Championship Wrestling, I would probably be in much better condition today. Imagine if all I had to do to my spiritual problems was a loud, ferocious monologue, an angry glare, and a few metal fold-up chairs. We could all be champions of faith if it were that easy. But of course it isn't, so we all have to learn how to fight spiritually. But, we have to *unlearn* the way we learned to fight in order to fight spiritually.

fight

Many of us grew up in families where the way to get your point across best was to raise your voice the loudest. Growing up, that's how things were in my home. And let me be clear about something: yelling families kind of have this stigma that they're really dysfunctional. That might be the case sometimes, but for sure not in all cases. *Every* family has *some* dysfunction that they have to work through. The quiet families are just as messed up as the loud ones. I'm not ashamed to tell you that in my home we sometimes yell, or *holler* (depending on where you live). It's just how we grew up, and at times it bubbles back up.

In the school yard, fights are won by being the strongest and having the most friends around you to back you up. It's kind of a gang mentality. Strength in numbers helps, but when it boils down to it, you had to be the strongest to win. Fights were won, sometimes before they even started, if you had enough friends to back you up. But whether it was strength in numbers, or just being the strongest person, winning the fight meant getting the at-a-boys, getting the respect. Even if you cheat while fighting – maybe you grab a jump rope and whip your opponent into submission – you at least got the respect of being the guy who will cheat to win.

Might makes right. This is the way we are taught to fight. It works for a lot of things in this world. Who's the strongest? Who has the bigger, better weapons? If we learned anything from the Cold War, the countries with the most nuclear weapons tended to influence everything on the planet. Mutually assured destruction is what kept the Soviet Union and the United States from ever firing a nuclear shot at each other for over forty years. As much as our hearts may want peace and justice to reign in this world, the reality is that as long as there is sin in the human heart, might makes right will continue to be our default fallback position. *We can't agree? I have the bigger guns, I have the most money, I can make you disappear from the map, so let's get on with things.* From the White House to the locker room, if all else fails, this is how we win in this world.

The kingdom of God, however, turns everything we know about fighting on its head. *The meek shall inherit the earth* (Matthew 5:5). For the longest time, I had no idea what that meant. My best idea actually came from *The Wizard of Oz* when Dorothy introduces herself to the Wizard as *Dorothy, the small and meek.* Otherwise, people just never used the word *meek* in their daily conversations. So I took that to mean that the small and pitiful would inherit the earth, therefore, Christians were supposed to be this crowd of people who shrunk back when challenged, never got into fights, always turned the other cheek, and basically wimped out when pushed.

There's a lot of wrong-headed thinking in that, but that's where I was for several years after becoming a Christian. I found myself ultimately frustrated. I hated conflict, but it's part of who we are as humans. When I would find myself angry, when I found myself wanting to fight back, I was at the same time feeling guilty. What was I supposed to do with my anger if the *meek* would inherit the earth? Anger

fight

didn't feel very meek to me because I had it all wrong on the meaning of meekness.

What about this one: *if you're struck on the right cheek, turn the other cheek* (Matthew 5:39). Or this one: *if you're holding anger against your brother, you're as guilty as a murderer* (Matthew 5:21-22). If we've been commanded to use these rules of engagement, how in the world are we supposed to survive in a system that hates us? If the world views victory through might makes right, then it looks like we're in big trouble.

At this moment in history, we're seeing the ultimate manifestation of the Christian philosophy on worldly conflict right before our eyes. As the forces of ISIS (Islamic State of Iraq and Syria) are on the rampage in the Middle-East, Christians are being rounded up by force, and told to renounce Christ or face death. Many have chosen death. Some have been murdered on camera for the whole world to see. Beheaded on the shores of the Mediterranean, twenty-one Christian men met Christ face to face at the hands of their extremist murderers.

Some of us have looked on with disbelief. Is that it? Do we just throw up our hands and surrender? Do we not take up arms to defend ourselves in the face of terrorists? I live in the rural Ozarks of Missouri, and I can tell you that many Christians I know are well armed. Some of their responses to the martyrdom of our brothers has been something to the tune of, *I'd rather go down in a blaze of bullets and take out as many of them as I can.* Can I be honest and say that I've had those same feelings? I believe it's important to think through what you will do in those situations where you are faced with either dying or taking a life in order to survive. What would I do in a situation where it was kill or be killed? What would you do?

Meekness: what does it look like in conflict? For sure, I don't live in a climate where my faith puts my life in danger. That could change, but for the time being the United States is still a safe place to be a Christian. I tell the men in my Thursday morning prayer group that we always tend to think about the extreme cases. *What if* . . . (fill in the blank)? But the truth is that conflict for the Christian isn't only when our *life, liberty, and pursuit of happiness* are threatened. In fact, most of the conflict we endure exists within the confines of our minds. That's where the fight begins. That's where much of it remains. And the times when it spills out into the world around us, even then much of it remains within.

The way we define meekness is to look at Jesus. He is the personification of meekness. Jesus is God. He is a member of the Trinity, the Godhead. He is the creative aspect of God. He is the Word, and God used his Word to speak all things *ex nihilo* (out of nothing) into existence. To say that Jesus is powerful would be an incredible understatement. Yet Jesus allowed himself to be crucified.

> For this reason the Father loves me, because I lay down my life that I may take it up again. No one takes it from me, but I lay it down of my own accord. I have

authority to lay it down, and I have authority to take it up again. This charge I have received from my Father. (John 10:17-18 ESV)

Jesus had the power to stop those who opposed him, yet he did not because a greater purpose would be served through his death. Meekness is having the power to change or affect your circumstances, yet restraining yourself for a greater purpose. When we deal with people, this should be our defining characteristic. Why? If someone wrongs me, or someone violates my rights or my property, what would be wrong with doing everything within my power to see justice served? As believers we should be cautious about allowing the *might makes right* philosophy of the world to control our responses. The war that Christians are engaged in is seldom what it seems.

> For we do not wrestle against flesh and blood, but against the rulers, against the authorities, against the cosmic powers over this present darkness, against the spiritual forces of evil in the heavenly places. (Ephesians 6:12 ESV)

Our enemy isn't the flesh and blood that we see before us. As deadly as extremist Muslims are toward Christians, Muslims are not the enemy. As much as we may feel like our government is increasingly against us, the government isn't the enemy. Homosexuals may have an agenda, but they aren't the enemy either. Neither are Democrats or Republicans for that matter. At worst, these men and women are tools of the enemy, but they are not enemies themselves. Satan fuels their ideologies and agendas by tempting their selfish desires and blinding them to the truth.

> In their case the god of this world [Satan] has blinded the minds of the unbelievers, to keep them from seeing the light of the gospel of the glory of Christ, who is the image of God. (2 Corinthians 4:4 ESV)
>
> But each person is tempted when he is lured and enticed by *his own desire*. Then desire when it has conceived gives birth to sin, and sin when it is fully grown brings forth death. (James 1:14-15 ESV, emphasis added)

When a Christian encounters opposition, the position taken should be one of, *God loves this person and doesn't desire that he or she perish.* If we could embrace that, it would forever change our interactions with people. I've been working through this for a long time in my life. There was a time where I wouldn't even spit on certain people if they were on fire. That's the kind of animosity that had built up from the hurts that had been piling up for years. But the more I started wrapping my heart around the Gospel and how to love both my neighbors and my enemies, I was able to let go of that animosity. God loves those guys. He desires that they know

fight

Jesus as Lord and Savior the same way I have. And if I love God they way I say I do, then I can't be angry with my enemies any more. In fact, I can't even really call them enemies any more. Just as I too was once blinded, people who are easy to label as enemies are likewise blinded and need our God to remove those blinders so they can see the light of the Gospel.

So back to the question at hand. How do we fight? If things aren't as they seem, and the flesh and blood in our face isn't the true enemy, how do we advance the kingdom of God? First, acknowledge *who* the real enemies of your soul are. All Christians have two principal enemies. The first one is obvious – Satan – but he isn't the most immediate enemy. There is another enemy who is more pressing. Who has let you down the most? Who has lied to you the most? What person has consistently been the biggest disappointment in your life? Which person has promised you more than anyone else, and subsequently broken those promises?

Take a look in the mirror. You are your own worst enemy. No one lies to you more than you. No one lets you down more than you. No one breaks promises to you more than you. No one derails your life more than you. Enemy number one in your battle is the man or woman in the mirror. For a long time, I struggled to think this through. I used to be one of those guys who blamed the Devil for everything. Bad day? Satan is clearly up to no good. Car not starting? Demons have afflicted my vehicle. Had an argument with my wife? Satan must be up in *her* business today . . . or mine, but probably hers.

Let's be clear, Satan *is* out to destroy me. Did he cause my car to not start? Did he provoke an argument between me and Radene? Probably not. When Jesus called Peter and Andrew, he said to them, *"Follow me, and I will make you fishers of men."* (Matthew 4:19 ESV). Not to be bested, Satan is also a fisher of men.

When I was younger, my sisters and I would sometimes spend the night with my cousins at my Uncle Sam's house. One of my favorite memories of this is going fishing with Uncle Sam. He loved fishing. I remember how he would set a trotline across an area of the water and leave it overnight. If you don't know what that is, a trotline is a long, heavy fishing line that's baited with hooks on short lines that hang down in the water at intervals along the main line. You stretch that out across a creek or a small cove on a pond or lake and leave it for several hours. Later, you come back and check your hooks. On a good day you can catch a lot of fish with one long trotline.

This is exactly how Satan fishes. He lays a trotline across your life. An old Puritan named Thomas Brooks says it like this: he fixes the bait, and hides the hook.[1] Then he waits. The success of his fishing depends entirely upon our lack of discernment. The lures are carefully selected. They play on our sinfulness. They are attractive to our flaws. The Devil's primary tactic is to entice what is already within us. That's why James says that we are *lured and enticed by [our] own desire* (James 1:14). Satan will never be held responsible for my failures. That judgment will fall on me alone. He may have used a clever bait, but whose choice was it to bite? Mine. I must take responsibility for myself, and own up to my failures before I can ever make any advance in this war. Too much of my early years of faith were spent blaming Satan for my own stupidity. By doing that, I was taking swings at the wrong guy. When you scapegoat someone on the outside for your problems, it enables you to ignore the mess on the inside where the real issues reside.

We take the war to ourselves first. In the mid nineties, when I was in college, I was still really young in my faith. I was zealous, but not very discerning. I ended up in a relationship with a young woman for about a year and a half. We loved each other, but I wasn't very mature through it all. The relationship became toxic to my spiritual life. We were both Christians, but we allowed things to go too far physically. This threw me into a spiritual tailspin. I was constantly feeling guilty and condemned, asking for forgiveness over and over, but also attempting to cover my tracks and maintain a certain appearance with my Christian friends. I was miserable lying to my friends and constantly coming to God with the same failures. It wasn't her fault, but for a while I blamed her. I thought she was the one making me miserable. I blamed her for being a temptress. Finally, we broke it off. It wasn't a clean break, and it took a little while for me to let go, but eventually it was over.

With a little distance from that relationship, my heart began to mend. But what I found in subsequent relationships that I attempted is that everything I blamed her for had followed me. God opened my eyes. I needed to stop scapegoating my issues onto others and deal with the mess that was within me. It wasn't the girls. It wasn't Satan. It was me! I may have been born again, but I still had a rotting corpse of sin walking around with me in my life.

> We know that our old self was crucified with him in order that the body of sin might be brought to nothing, so that we would no longer be enslaved to sin. (Romans 6:6 ESV)

The day you are born again the old self, that you were, dies. That's what is symbolized in baptism. When you go under the water, that is the death of your old self. When you come up out of the water, that is the new self that has been newly born by the Holy Spirit.

> For one who has died has been set free from sin. Now if we have died with Christ, we believe that we will also live with him. (Romans 6:7-8 ESV)

The death of the old self means that you are no longer enslaved by its desires. You don't have to obey the cravings of your old life any more because the new self that has been born within you possesses the power, through the Holy Spirit, to deny those old desires and cravings. For me, recognizing this truth is immensely helpful. I already possess the power to say *no* to my old desires, and say *yes* to the new desires of my new self. It's just a matter of choosing which desire I will feed.

The problem is that though the old self is dead, he is kind of *undead*. I despise the infatuation our culture has taken to zombies, but I'm going to borrow from it because it makes for an excellent illustration. As a believer, your old self is just like a zombie. It is dead, yet it's still walking around. It's dead, but it still has an appetite. It's dead, but if you allow it, it can still consume your life.

> Let not sin therefore reign in your mortal body, to make you obey its passions. Do not present your members to sin as instruments for unrighteousness, but present yourselves to God as those who have been brought from death to life, and your members to God as instruments for righteousness. (Romans 6:12-13 ESV)

It really does boil down to which self are you going to feed: the new self, born by the Holy Spirit, or the old self, dead but undead? Both have appetites. Feeding either of them will lead them to greater appetites. Feeding the new self will lead to a deepening appetite for the things of God. Feeding the old self will only increase its appetite for more sin. Feeding the new self leads to life because it is alive. Feeding the old self leads to death because it is dead.

> For those who live according to the flesh set their minds on the things of the flesh, but those who live according to the Spirit set their minds on the things of the Spirit. For to set the mind on the flesh is death, but to set the mind on the Spirit is life and peace. (Romans 8:5-6 ESV)

When you take the war to yourself, you begin to realize that your sin is the only sin that you have time and strength to deal with. Making war against your old-self-zombie is a full-time engagement. All of your sins begin to look like planks and everyone else's sins look like specs in comparison. Do you know how to know when you've stopped fighting? You know you've stopped fighting when everyone else's sin looks like planks and your own sin looks like specs. You know you've stopped fighting when you find yourself constantly believing you have the moral high ground. You're disengaged from drawing close to God, which is inherently a battle, and engaged in feeding the zombie which requires almost no effort. Relearning how to fight means learning to keep yourself in the crosshairs instead of others.

Just as important as the *who*, we also need to know *where*. Where does this battle happen? There isn't just one front for this war. Spiritual war happens on every possible front in our lives. We engage in this war on five different fronts: socially, economically, physically, emotionally, and spiritually. They are all connected, so if one is suffering they all suffer. Let me briefly address each one.

fight

There is a social aspect to warring against your sin. Essentially this means that your chosen company of friends will play a role in the war. I mentioned in the last chapter that a large portion of the book of Proverbs deals with wisdom in choosing friends. The Apostle Paul instructs us in 1 Corinthians 15:33, *"Bad company ruins good morals."* (ESV). The book of Hebrews reminds us that we should not forsake assembling together for worship (Hebrews 10:25). There are fifty-nine *one-anothers* (love one another, accept one another, etc.) in the New Testament. If you are out of whack within the social aspect of your life, you are leaving an area of your life vulnerable to attack.

There is an economic aspect of spiritual war. It's often said that Jesus spoke about money more than he spoke about hell. In fact, Jesus spoke about money more than he spoke about any other topic except the kingdom of God. Perhaps no other statement about the economic aspect of spiritual war is more comprehensive than this: *"For where your treasure is, there your heart will be also,"* (Matthew 6:21 ESV). Many a preacher has said that you can tell where a person's heart is by looking at their checkbook. It's true but only because Jesus said it first. Are you being a good manager of the finances and resources that God has entrusted to you? Are you generous because God has been generous to you? Are you a *cheerful giver* (2 Corinthians 9:7)? If your economics aren't underpinned with biblical counsel, if you are poorly managing what God has entrusted to you, there will be a place for Satan to gain an advantage.

There is a physical aspect of spiritual war. When the body is weak, there is less ability to resist temptation. When you're weak physically from illness, you will be more inclined to take the path of least resistance when you're tempted. This is why people are grumpy when they're tired. When you're tired or sick, it's just easier to be a grump because being nice takes more effort. It's the same in spiritual life. When we're exhausted, giving in to temptation will always be the easier path. King Solomon penned this in Psalm 127:

> It is in vain that you rise up early and go late to rest, eating the bread of anxious toil; for he gives to his beloved sleep. (Psalm 127:2 ESV)

Sleep is a blessing! If you don't get enough of it, you will suffer physically. This should be common sense, but so many of us run ourselves into the ground with work. Solomon calls that *eating the bread of anxious toil*. Basically, when you refuse to sleep because you *need* to work, you are refusing to rest in God's sovereignty so you take matters into your own hand. Sickness eventually follows having a weakened body from constant fatigue which makes you more vulnerable on the spiritual war front. If you want to fight effective spiritual war, you must take care of yourself physically.

There's an emotional aspect of spiritual war. This one is closely tied to the social aspect because few things mess with your emotions more than your relationships. However, the emotional aspect of spiritual war runs deeper than the social. What kind of person are you emotionally? Do you tend to be fairly level in your emotional responses, or do you tend toward extremes? When you get sucker punched by situations, what is your knee jerk reaction? Are you one who wants to punch back, or are you one who withdraws to nurse your wounds? Are you prone to depression? Are you the life of the party? Knowing who you are and understanding the pitfalls of being your type of person is crucial. Look again to the Proverbs; there are numerous references on how to handle your emotions in a godly way. But most important, one aspect of the fruit of the Spirit is *self-control* (Galatians 5:22-23) which means you have a firm grasp of your emotions. Being a person who gives his or her emotions free reign with no restraint will give Satan *huge* opportunities.

Finally, there is obviously a spiritual aspect to spiritual war. Now I could get into a lengthy discussion about demons and angels and how they have their roles, but there's one problem with that. Much of the stuff you read and hear about angels and demons has very little basis in what the Bible teaches. In fact, in terms of sheer volume, what the Bible does say about angels and demons still doesn't amount to as much as you might think. We do know some things, but what we do know for sure tends to leave us with lots more questions. Therefore, the spiritual aspect of our fight needs to start with knowing the Holy Spirit who has been given to everyone born into God's kingdom. Cultivate the relationship with the Holy Spirit within. Immerse yourself in the Word of God.

Understand that the Holy Spirit will never tell you something or ask you to do something that contradicts what God has already revealed in the Word. Jesus said this about the Holy Spirit and what he has come to do.

> When the Spirit of truth comes, he will *guide you into all the truth*, for he will not speak on his own authority, but *whatever he hears he will speak*, and he will *declare to you the things that are to come*. (John 16:13 ESV, emphasis added)

The Holy Spirit's role in our fight is to show the truth, to speak to us exactly what the Father tells him to speak, and to tell us of things that are coming. Getting to know his voice means the difference in blessing and cursing, life and death. He guides us into all truth, and we can know that what he says is from the Father. But what about that last one: *declare to you the things that are to come.*

I am not a prophet, I've never received a direct word of prophecy about future events, so you might consider my experience with this to be novice at best. However, I don't think what Jesus said was limited to direct revelation of future events. I've had several times in my life where I sensed the Holy Spirit placing an urgency in my spirit to *get ready.* For what? All I knew to do was to push in harder toward Jesus. Be extra aware, extra diligent in my disciplines. I've recorded some of these moments in my journals. In 2009, I received that familiar *get ready* urgency, and a year later God was moving my family to a new church in a different city and state. He makes us ready for the future. Knowing his voice is absolutely important to fighting spiritually.

Lastly, once you engage in this fight, you will discover something incredibly important. *You can't do this.* You and I are not naturally equipped to fight this kind of war. We're not smart enough, we're not strong enough, we're incapable of sustaining ourselves in the prolonged nature of spiritual war. As important as knowing the *who* and *where* of the war, it isn't enough. Now you need to learn *how* to fight the enemy. The *how* has way less to do with you and me, and way more to do with Jesus. All of that stuff I just laid on you really is impossible in your own strength. How you fight is to let Jesus do your fighting. My effort in this is to simply trust and obey. The old hymn got it right: *Trust and obey, for there's no other way, to be happy in Jesus, than to trust and obey.*[2] I *trust* that the cross was enough. That his death on the cross was the mortal blow to Satan. I *trust* that the resurrection was the mortal blow to death and its power over me. I *obey* because he loved me enough to die for me. I *obey* because I *trust* that his plan for me is perfect. When I'm doing those two things, Jesus' victory over Satan becomes my victory.

Friends, this has taken me years to *start* grasping. By no means have I mastered it. Embracing the fight has been a fight. There remains in me a dark streak of sloth that would rather just let things roll off my back than engage in any battles, because I have never felt like much of a fighter. But thankfully, in God's kingdom, the fight isn't even my fight. The battle belongs to the Lord. That doesn't mean I don't have a role, but it does mean that my role is only as a supporting actor. God wants people to see Jesus doing the fighting, not Shane. Learning to let him fight through me has been both a hard lesson and huge blessing, and it is the responsibility of all believers to relearn how to fight. In fact, it's so important that in Revelation, the bloodiest, most violent book of his Word, God says this toward the end, and with it I will close this chapter.

> The one who *conquers* will have this heritage, and I will be his God and he will be my son. (Revelation 21:7 ESV, emphasis added)

Conquerors are *fighters*.

References
1. Thomas Brooks, *Precious Remedies Against Satan's Devices*, Banner of Truth Trust, Carlisle, Pennsylvania, 1968.
2. Daniel Brink Towner, John Henry Sammis, *When We Walk With The Lord (Trust and Obey)*, Public Domain.

our victor

One of the most memorable moments in my life was my senior year of high school. Our basketball team went to the state tournament. We were good. We had talented players who knew the game. We were in the semifinals playing Wheeler, MS, and the game was close. Plus, Wheeler was a huge rival team for us. We had a history of meeting up and playing some incredible basketball. Sometimes at state, sometimes in the regular season. I guess it's safe to say we hated each other. Anyway, I think it was the last two minutes and we were trailing by a couple points. I was a statistician for the team, so I'm sitting on the bench, clenching my clipboard with a death grip. Wheeler had possession. As they brought the ball down the court, our team was in a full-on press. We were sticking to them like glue. Then it happened. The whistle blew, and one of the referees called foul. There's always that moment between the whistle and the call where you have a moment of hope that the call will be in your favor. The way I remember is that this was a really long moment.

In basketball there are defensive fouls and offensive fouls. Most of the fouls called are defensive because the are committed by the players trying to defend their goal. But sometimes there are offensive fouls where the team with possession of the ball can be too aggressive in their drive to make a basket. One of the strategies of the game is for the team on defense to lure the offense into committing a foul. One of those fouls is called a charge, named because it's when an offensive player *charges* over a defensive player, running him over. If you're a good defensive player, you can position yourself to take a charge, get the foul called, and regain possession of the ball. As Wheeler brought the ball down the court, one of our guys positioned himself for a charge. He took it. The whistle blew.

The foul was called on us, not Wheeler. Unfortunately, if you don't do the charge right, the foul can get turned around and called on you as blocking, which simply means you were illegally blocking the path of an opponent. Questionable call? You bet! But what made it worse is that it allowed Wheeler to score some free throws, giving them a lead that we simply couldn't overcome in the remaining time. We left the Jackson Coliseum that night wounded and hurt. I won't lie, I cried. That was our class' last chance to win gold at state, and we felt robbed. We played a good game. A questionable call threw the game to Wheeler.

Taking a charge is always a risk. Sometimes you're successful and the charge is called. Sometimes, you don't quite do it right, and the call is blocking. Sometimes nothing is called at all, and you have to get up off the floor and hustle back to your position. In this case, we lost and it cost us the game. Occasionally I look back and wonder if that was the best move. Would we have fared better to force them into a hard shot and miss? But then again, they had the lead so they didn't have to really score anymore points if they simply ran out the clock. Maybe trying to take a charge was one of the best options for us. I ran this scenario through my head for days after that game. What would've made the difference for us to have won that game?

In truth, it's never that simple. It wasn't that single moment that determined the outcome of the game. What if we had made more free throws from earlier in the game? What if we hadn't made quite so many turnovers? There were a multitude of ways that we could have won the game that would've made that one questionable call kind of unimportant. That basketball game was decided by the sum of our team's performance in the whole game, not just by a bad call at the end. It's easier to blame that one moment, but a little perspective always reveals a string of moments that line up to make what happened at the end.

There have been times in my life where I felt defined by the moment. Many of the moments I've shared with you have been some of those times. Bullied, loser, rejected, awkward, people pleaser: when you're in the moment, it's difficult to see beyond. Fortunately, none of those moments were the final verdict. And truly, the final verdict hasn't been handed down yet. The buzzer hasn't gone off yet. I'm still here. I'm still making choices. I'm still being transformed. The final verdict won't be made until I stand before King Jesus and receive my judgment and commendation. When my works are tested by fire, whatever survives that fire will be rewarded.

> For no one can lay a foundation other than that which is laid, which is Jesus Christ. Now if anyone builds on the foundation with gold, silver, precious stones, wood, hay, straw—each one's work will become manifest, for the Day will disclose it, because it will be revealed by fire, and the fire will test what sort of work each one has done. If the work that anyone has built on the foundation survives, he will receive a reward. If anyone's work is burned up, he will suffer loss, though he himself will be saved, but only as through fire. (1 Corinthians 3:11-15 ESV)

Who knows what will survive those fires of judgment? I've spent *much* of my adult life serving the church in different capacities. I'm certain that a good number of the things I did in the beginning won't survive those fires as they were soiled by selfish motives. As the Holy Spirit has continually molded me into a new creation, many of those selfish motives have gradually been nudged out. Are they gone? Of course not! I hear their cries every day and I do my best to starve them. I only regret that I'm not more successful in that! Unfortunately, I still feed the old-self-zombie far too much. However, the good news is God has promised to finish the good work he began in me (Philippians 1:6). I won't be the same guy one year from today that I am today, guaranteed!

There's an important lesson that every believer needs to let sink into their souls. Your past doesn't have to cripple you. All these events that I've shared with you from my life only cripple me if I allow them to continue defining my present. I didn't share these things with the world so I could somehow get a therapeutic benefit from hashing out my feelings about my past. Friends, I have shared these things with you to help you see that God can take anyone and transform their life. I should be a statistic. Chris Rock famously said once that if you call your grandma, *mom*, and call your mom by her first name, you're going to jail! That was my story! Hallelujah! God intercepted my statistic! And not only did he intercept my statistic, he flipped it and has used it to grow me.

> And we know that for those who love God *all things* work together *for good*, for those who are called according to his purpose. (Romans 8:28 ESV, emphasis added)

God uses *all things* to grow his children. What are *all things*? What is the *good* that God is working toward? *All things* means what it says. Everything that happens in your life – good or bad – God uses. That means from your birth, to your death, God uses all of the circumstances and events of your life for good. That's a hard one to swallow. All of that bullying? All of the unkind words? All of my selfishness? All of my bad choices? God uses that too? *All things*: you cannot escape what God has said. Honestly, my experiences have been kind of pale compared to many. I have Christian friends who have had abortions. I have Christian friends who *convinced* their girlfriends to get abortions. I have friends who have been drug addicted, alcohol addicted, sex addicted, raped, molested, abandoned, physically abused, and they all are Christians today, set free and recovering. I have believing friends who are currently going through cancer and everything that entails. What about them? *All things*? How can I say that God uses *all things* for their good?

I'm not saying it. God is. What I've done in my life is keep that track on repeat. He uses all things. He uses all things. He uses all things. I constantly remind myself of this truth because even having been saved for twenty-three years, I still find myself doing things that grieve the Holy Spirit within. When I mess things up, I have to remember he uses all things and I get back up, confess, repent, and keep pushing upward. It's not a justification for sinning, it's a remembrance that my sins aren't bigger than my God. If he can take my failures and use them for my good, then he is greater than anything or anyone that tempts me. Remember Joseph?

> As for you, you meant evil against me, but God meant it for good . . . (Genesis 50:20 ESV)

There it is again. The word *good*. Joseph said it. Paul said it. What is this *good* that God is working toward in us? Is it a good life? Is it a good reputation? Is it a good circumstance? There's a lot of thought out there that God will pay off all your bills, bless you with a well-paying job, bless you with a nice home, a nice car, and a fat tax refund every year. Don't misunderstand me; God can do those things. But is that the *good* that he's talking about in Romans? Is that the *good* that Joseph was talking about? Joseph went through hell by the acre to get to where he was when he uttered those words. Paul also endured hell on earth, beaten and left for dead, shipwrecked, imprisoned, persecuted, ran out of town, for most of his adult life, yet he wrote that God intended those things for good. I want to explain this to you, but I'll need to lead you on a short journey to get there. Stay with me, we're almost home!

John the Baptist said that Jesus will baptize us *with the Holy Spirit and with fire* (Matthew 3:11). What is fire baptism? What does fire represent? Fire represents the judgment of God.

> But who can endure the day of his coming, and who can stand when he appears? For he is like a *refiner's fire* and like fullers' soap. He will sit as a refiner and purifier of silver, and *he will purify the sons of Levi and refine them like gold and silver*, and they will bring offerings in righteousness to the LORD. (Malachi 3:2-3 ESV, emphasis added)

> In this you rejoice, though now for a little while, if necessary, you have been grieved by various trials, so that the tested genuineness of your faith—more precious than gold that perishes though it is *tested by fire*—may be found to result in praise and glory and honor at the revelation of Jesus Christ. (1 Peter 1:6-7 ESV, emphasis added)

This judgment, like mentioned earlier, tests the quality of our faith and works. But this judgment doesn't only come after we have died, it tests us in this life as well. Malachi refers to the fire of the Day of the Lord. Peter refers to the fire of trials that we endure as we live out our faith. We are baptized by fire, or into suffering. Economic hardship? War? Drought? Disease? Everyone suffers these, but the fire that is judgment for the unbeliever is refining for the believer! God uses *all things* for the *good* of those who love him. What are these trials producing in us?

> For those whom he foreknew he also predestined to be *conformed to the image of his Son,* in order that he might be the firstborn among many brothers. (Romans 8:29 ESV, emphasis added)

These trials are shaping us into people who live like, talk like, behave like Jesus Christ. The baptism by fire is a promise of trials that will refine us and change us into the people that God desires. It isn't some hyper-charismatic ecstatic experience. Fire baptism is a baptism into suffering. It is an immersion into refining judgment.

How does God use all things, good or bad? He uses them to refine us into worshipers. Have you made mistakes? Your mistakes will either push you further into darkness, or push you toward the light. When God calls you into salvation, he turns the orientation of your troubled past to push you toward the light! He isn't one to waste a single moment of your life. He can take anything from your life and use it to bring glory to himself! Whether it's something from way back before you knew Christ, or something currently happening today as a believer, God's plan for that suffering is to draw out the impurities in your life like a refiner's fire. Expect hard things. But also expect God to do amazing things with your hard things!

A friend of mine, Karen, has endured breast cancer and emerged healthy on the other side. She was very public with her journey through it. It was quite serious, but she held tightly to Jesus through it. She suffered like all cancer patients do. Loss of hair, horrible chemotherapy, radiation, physically weakened, weakened immunity, to say she endured much is an understatement. If she had gone through that without knowing Jesus, it would've been completely random, devoid of purpose, just a roll of Mother Nature's dice. But because she loves God and knows his Son, God has taken that struggle and turned it into something that has purpose. Karen has written a book, *The Pink Duck*, that chronicles her journey through cancer. God is using Karen's suffering to shine a light on Jesus that wouldn't have been possible without a hard journey through breast cancer.

How do you view your suffering? Do you view it as bad luck? Some people chalk it up to karma. Others just see it as a bad fortune. The believer should never view their suffering in such categories. Even the sufferings that are self-inflicted, God can use for a redemptive purpose. James, the brother of Jesus, wrote this:

> Count it all joy, my brothers, when you meet trials of various kinds, for you know that the testing of your faith produces steadfastness. And let steadfastness have its full effect, that you may be perfect and complete, lacking in nothing. (James 1:2-4 ESV)

This does not mean *enjoy your trial*. No one enjoys suffering. There hasn't been a single moment of my suffering that I enjoyed. When I was in the middle of ridicule, or when I was going through relationship troubles, I never sat back and said, "This isn't so bad." No! I was desperately trying to find a way out! The temptation for me, and I think all of us, is to find a shortcut out of suffering. That's not to say that we should linger in our suffering because it's somehow holier or more purifying. No way! But the shortcut often is a compromise. You can make a pretty good argument that had I given in to my anger and fought my bullies, things might have been different. But what of the command to remain sinless in our anger (Ephesians 4:26)? And what kind of person would I be today if things had been different? There's always a compromise in a shortcut. Endure your trial. The joy doesn't come from the trial. The joy comes from the outcome of the trial!

The outcome is the *good* that God is working toward in his children. Your attitude toward your suffering will make the difference in how you live your life and how you make decisions. Will you continue to see your suffering as unjust? As undeserving? As the mood swings of a capricious God? Or will you see them as refining fires that are transforming you into the likeness of Jesus Christ? Christian, you must keep your eyes fixed upon Jesus at all times, or else when trials come you'll be tempted to see them as the world sees them. How? It's the question that I have asked over and over as I've journeyed. The answer is simple and profound.

Christ is our victory. None of the strides I have made over the things I've shared with you have come because I'm somehow smarter or stronger than the average bear. Had it been up to me to overcome, I can confidently say that you and I would not be sharing this moment right now. I imagine that if it had been left up to me I would have shrunk back and become somewhat of a recluse. Naturally, I'm quite introverted. I still am, but I have Christ within me working to strengthen me and grow me in ways that I wouldn't have grown on my own. Christ is winning these struggles for me. Christ is taking everything I've shared with you and against nature is creating a man that never would've existed otherwise. God is in the business of calling things into existence that do not exist (Romans 4:17). The man I am today, and the man I will be tomorrow had no chance to exist had it not been for Jesus Christ. Every victory belongs to Jesus. Each moment of growth flows from the victory that Jesus won in his death and resurrection. That's how we win.

Everyone has adversity. In a world where everything is fundamentally broken, the struggle is to breathe life into dead things. It's a struggle that is common to all of us. Think about it: from the moment we are born, we are on a journey that will end with our death. The time we spend in between those moments is spent trying to pour more life into the life that we have. The phrase *you only live once* is the catch phrase of the day. YOLO! So live your life to the max, do everything you can to experience, to extend, to enliven the life that you have now because you only have one. But we're ultimately trying to resuscitate a corpse that was dead from the moment it was born. Adversity comes and reminds us that everything is broken. Life itself is bent toward destruction. At the core, life is really more like *Lord of the Flies* than it is *The Brady*

Bunch. When you eat dinner with your family, the harsh reality is that one person at the table will live to see everyone else at the table dead. We know this instinctively, so we do everything we can to take our minds away from that truth. We desperately try to breathe life into the people and things we love, but in the end we don't have that kind of power.

This is where Jesus steps in. Because Jesus has defeated death, his victory serves to defeat death and destruction wherever it may be found. Christ enters in, and brings into existence this new man, made from the ashes of the old one, and breathes in eternal life. In that moment, every mistake I ever made, every hurt, every rejection, all of my poor choices, all of my character flaws are breathed on by the Holy Spirit of God and they instantly receive new life! What used to be regret, is now redeemed. What once condemned me now cooperates with me. Those parts of my story that once brought me shame have been redeemed and instead of condemning me they now cooperate with me in spreading the Gospel. Whatever hurt I've been through, and however I am hurt in the future, it all now has the glorious purpose of demonstrating how Jesus Christ redeems the fallen and brings dead things to life!

If you've been a believer, even for a short time, and you find that you can't seem to find victory over past hurts, past choices, consider this: you're searching and fighting out of your own understanding and strength. You need a change of perspective. You don't need to win anything. Jesus has already won! You only need to realize this and adjust your thinking and living accordingly! Since Christ is our victory, we can live boldly! We can live as a victor and not a victim! We have received *everything* we need in order to live this victorious life in the Holy Spirit (Galatians 5:22-23; 2 Peter 1:3-4). We only need to change our thinking through immersing ourselves in the Word (Romans 12:2) and fellowshipping with the Spirit of God within (John 16:13). Christ, our Victor, leads us in triumphal procession.

> But thanks be to God, who in Christ always leads us in triumphal procession, and through us spreads the fragrance of the knowledge of him everywhere. (2 Corinthians 2:14 ESV)

Perhaps you're not a believer, and against all odds, you have endured to the end of this book and sense that you need the forgiveness I've spoken of many times. Jesus Christ made a way for anyone to receive forgiveness who would humble themselves by repenting of their sins, and believing that Jesus Christ is Lord, trusting him alone for salvation. The Gospel is simple. Jesus Christ, the only Son of God, conceived by the Holy Spirit, born of the virgin Mary, lived a perfect sinless life in thought, word, and deed. He was wrongfully crucified and died a sinner's death (the death you and I deserve). Being sinless, he was undeserving of death, so God the Father raised him up on the third day, forever defeating death and the grave, and proving that he is who he said he was, the Son of God! He ascended to heaven, and he waits until the appointed moment for his return, when he will come to judge the living and the dead. That was a mouthful, and it probably stirs a lot of questions, but if you believe these things about Jesus, confess and repent of your sins, and trust him alone for salvation, you will be saved!

> If you confess with your mouth that Jesus is Lord and believe in your heart that God raised him from the dead, you will be saved. For with the heart one believes and is justified, and with the mouth one confesses and is saved. (Romans 10:9-10 ESV)

There's no secret chant, no special prayer to pray, you only need to express these things to the Lord in your own words. It's simple, just begin a conversation with God. You might feel silly, you might feel like a lune, but that's ok. Faith can feel awkward because you're trusting something invisible. But it is the prayer of faith that God will hear, and upon that faith, he will give you the righteousness of Christ, and completely forgive you!

One more story, and then I'm done. When I was born, I was really sick. I had deadly respiratory issues. My family has told me time and time again that the doctors told them they had done all they could do. I was in a croup tent, struggling to breathe and my future was uncertain. Then our family chiropractor paid a visit. He adjusted my infant spine and immediately I began recovering! Buzz, our chiropractor, was a family friend, and for all intents and purposes, he saved my life. I might have never made it out of that hospital had it not been for Buzz doing his chiropractic magic that day. Because of that miracle, as I grew up my family would occasionally regale me with the tale and tell me that God had a plan for my life.

It was hard to believe. For all of the bullying and rejection, the idea that God had a plan for my life was difficult to swallow, especially as a young teen. But the truth is, his plan for my life includes my pain. He didn't cause it, but he sure doesn't waste it. God doesn't waste your pain. Suffering might seem like God's one mistake. It might seem like the detail of creation that slipped by his notice. When you're hurting, you can't fathom how any of it can be useful. Here's the truth: God didn't create suffering; it wasn't a part of his original design. Pain and suffering is something we brought upon ourselves when we sinned and broke fellowship with our Creator. But God's genius is that he takes our pain, and uses it as a cosmic megaphone to call our attention back to him.

Let God use your pain. The only way your suffering will ever count for anything meaningful is if you let God use it for his purposes. Otherwise, your suffering is just random bad luck in an aimless, chance existence. He wants to give you new life. Christian? Unbeliever? The response is the same. Turn your heart and gaze to Jesus, the Author and Finisher of our faith and he *will* save. He *will* bring the dead to life. And you *will* never be the same again.

in closing

It's been almost a year since I started composing this book. I've spent the last week or two reviewing, looking back over my shoulder, trying to make sure everything says what it needs to say. I've had some incredible people come along side me to review, edit, theologize, encourage, and offer correction and suggestions. I'm extremely grateful. I hope that one day I can do something for them that helps them in a similar magnitude of help. I couldn't have done this without you.

Digging into your past isn't always a pleasant journey. In the course of this excavation, I've had friends send me old pictures from my college days (and they had no idea what I've been doing, it was just a coincidence). I've even found some of my own old photos, some from high school, some from college, some from early childhood. Some of them were even from before the adoption. Can I be honest? I look at some of those old college photos and I don't even know who that guy is anymore. But then again, I know that guy really well. It gives me a knot in my stomach when I remember. Why was I so foolish in so many ways? Why didn't I listen better? Why did I try so hard for the approval of people I haven't seen in over twenty years? What would my life look like if I had made some different choices? You can truly drive yourself insane dwelling on the hypotheticals of *what might've been*.

The hypotheticals don't matter. The only way you can truly let go of them is by accepting that even though your journey is rife with mistakes, with fumbles, with errors, with sin, it doesn't matter: today is the day of salvation. The Apostle Paul wrote to the Corinthians, *"Behold, now is the favorable time; behold, now is the day of salvation,"* (2 Corinthians 6:2b, ESV). Today can be the moment where you make the choice that will transform all those mistakes, all those sins, all those fumbles from your past life from weights that sink you to the bottom of the ocean, to sails that Jesus uses to move you toward the shores of that glorious country where there are no more tears and pain, and where sin is a distant memory instead of a present reality. Your pain isn't a mistake. Your suffering is a vehicle through which God can demonstrate his limitless might and amazing grace and love.

Look at the woman caught in adultery from John chapter eight. All of her accusers stood holding stones. Jesus however knelt down in the dirt to meet her. She was caught in the act. Jesus never denies this, but he meets her with mercy, and at her lowest moment of shame and humiliation, she finds salvation. What more do you need to know? One

in closing

day he will come as Judge, but for now salvation is offered and he is our Advocate.

The details of your life are what they are; you can't change them. But Jesus can enter in and take the mess that you believe your life is and *recreate* you into a new man or woman who never would've existed otherwise. Dead people can't change anything on their own. They're dead. But Jesus, who calls the dead to life, can call you out of your deadness and give you a new life. You only need to trust him for salvation. You cannot save yourself, and to receive salvation, you have to abandon all of your own efforts and simply trust that Jesus is your only hope for salvation.

How can this be done? It actually isn't rocket science. The Bible tells us that it's very simple.

> because, if you confess with your mouth that Jesus is Lord and believe in your heart that God raised him from the dead, you will be saved. (Romans 10:9 ESV)

There's an element of confession, which means you must speak. Speak what? Some people call it a *sinner's prayer* but at its core it means to confess to God that you believe Jesus Christ is the Lord of all. Confession also means you repent of the sin in your life. To repent is to turn away from the things in your life that displease God and embrace things that do.

Then there's an element of belief. You believe in your heart, not your head, that God raised Jesus from the dead. That means you belief he's alive right now at the emotional center of your life. With every emotion in your being, you believe that Jesus Christ is just as alive right now as you are. It's far more than intellectual belief. It's more than a wish, or a hope. It's a reality just as real and constant to you as the rising and setting of the sun. You know it's true in your heart, even though your eyes can't confirm.

This is what it means to be saved. To have a mouth that repents and confesses Jesus, and to have a heart that has intertwined every emotion, every feeling in your life with the reality that Jesus Christ is alive today because God raised him from the dead. And once you're his, once you're born again into this saved life; life as you knew it will forever be different. You'll never look at your past again the same way. You'll never dream of the future the same way. And your present will be lived in a power that you never had before.

www.ingramcontent.com/pod-product-compliance
Lightning Source LLC
Chambersburg PA
CBHW060157050426
42446CB00013B/2870